SEVEN

SEVEN

THE DEADLY SINS AND THE BEATITUDES

JEFF COOK

ZONDERVAN®

ZONDERVAN.com/
AUTHORTRACKER
follow your favorite authors

ZONDERVAN®

Library of Congress Cataloging-in-Publication Data

Cook, Jeff, 1976-.
    Seven : the deadly sins and the Beatitudes / Jeff Cook.
        p.   cm.
    Includes bibliographical references.
    ISBN   978-0-310-27817-7 (softcover)
    1. Beatitudes — Criticism, interpretation, etc. 2. Deadly sins. I. Title.
  BT382.C64   2008
  241.5'3 — dc22   2008009418

Interior design by Beth Shagene

Printed in the United States of America

08 09 10 11 12 13 14 • 23 22 21 20 19 18 17 16 15 14 13 12 11 10 9 8 7 6 5 4 3 2 1

To Augie and Becket.
May you taste and enjoy the fruit
of heaven all around you.

CONTENTS

INTRODUCTION

HOLES IN
A GOOD WORLD

Between us and heaven or hell there is only life half-way,
the most fragile thing in the world.
BLAISE PASCAL

THE BEETLE WAS AN INCREDIBLE PLACE. IT USED TO BE THE COFFEE-drinking, Parliament-smoking, open-till-3:00 a.m. lounge next to the university. The lonely gathered at the Beetle at night. The homeless sat at the Beetle when there was nowhere else to sit. The Beetle had that vibe of posh college elitism mixed with a come-as-you-are indifference. It had flair. It had character. But when the city of Greeley decided to ban smoking in restaurants, the Beetle couldn't last.

The building had sat empty for almost two years when we began renting the space. It was the perfect size for a small church like ours. The Beetle still had much of its former comfort and nostalgic smell, and of course there was the upside-down VW Bug hanging from the front of the building. Black floors, tin walls, and gorgeous wood ceilings, the Beetle was a work of art, and we weren't the only ones who loved it.

The week that the people of Atlas began preparing the space and painting the walls, nearly thirty people came through its doors. Each one of them walked in looking for a familiar face, and they all asked the same question: "Hey, is the Beetle opening up again?" Of course, this was an opportunity to shake hands, introduce ourselves, and be welcoming. And, of course, no one cared.

"Actually, we're a church group that's renting the space," we would say. "We have drinks on the counter if you'd like to come in and have one."

Without exception, our guests' faces would drop. They would politely decline and turn toward the door, some with a respectfully muted curse as they stepped back onto the sidewalk. It was as though our church had taken something very valuable from them, something the people on Sixteenth Street had cherished, and was making it into a specialty shop for religious people.

On the night Atlas had its first gathering in the Beetle, we heard a collective groan from all of our neighbors. Sixteenth Street was once a well-loved strip of restaurants, bookstores, and music shops, but there just wasn't any life there anymore. Only the anticorporate idealists kept the few remaining shops in business, and in their eyes we were most unwelcome. We were just another sign that Sixteenth Street was dying.

That was two years ago. Last Friday, the forty or so folks of Atlas drew a crowd of a few thousand people onto Sixteenth Street for a block party. Some of the businesses next to us ran out of stock and shut down early that evening, not realizing how big the event would be. I saw at least five mullets, freshly shaven by the girls at the hair salon who were giving them away for free. My wife and some friends got new piercings at the tattoo shop. College students and locals erupted in protest when we had to shut down the main stage at 10:00 p.m. because, yes, we had to follow the noise ordinances. Yes, we know that "Paradise City" is a crowd favorite that can go on forever. And yes, we're aware that nothing good like this ever happens in Greeley, but the friendly police officers near the sound booth asked us to stop. We invited everyone off the street and into the Beetle, which quickly filled to standing room only. The music played on until 2:00 a.m.

When I went for my second beer that night, I introduced myself to the owner of the Crabtree Brewery. I asked for their wheat ale — one of the finest in Colorado — and he said they were out. I asked for the brown, which is a fine choice as well, but they were out of that too. They still had a ginger, he said.

"You sold out of beer?" I asked after trying a sample.

"Yeah, my family will be able to buy groceries this month because of this thing."

Occasionally, the planets align in bizarre patterns, prayers are taken as an opportunity for God to be mischievous — and standing in the middle of the beer garden, the local brewmaster looked at me and said, "I'm so glad your church is here. You bring so much life to this part of town."

Businesses are closing all around us. The Mexican food restaurant shut its doors last summer. Kimbrall's Music moved away. The only store that seems to thrive on Sixteenth Street is Mellow Yellow, the head shop next to us, where they carry a fine assortment of bongs, incense, and handmade clothing. Sixteenth Street was once filled with life, but now empty windows and For Rent signs decorate seven or so buildings on the strip. Yet for one night in early September, Sixteenth Street was the place to be in northern Colorado. The block party was a sign of things that could be. It was a symbol of hope for building owners and nostalgic workers who had almost given up.

I teach philosophy across the street, and the next day I spoke with my students — many of whom normally look for any reason to get out of this town and head over to Boulder or Fort Collins. They all knew something special had happened. "It just felt like everything worked," they said, "like this was how things should be on the drag next to the university."

The evening was remarkable because the people of Atlas took something that was dead and made it alive again, and for that night, at least, all who came out witnessed a resurrection.

Scraping Aside What Was Good

I grew up in a small mountain town in Colorado, a few miles from the best skiing in the world, yet distant enough that cows were the backbone of our local economy. The sharp hills and tree groves along my drive to school were striking pieces of scenery. The world's best photographers often capture the mountains near us. Locals rightly call it "God's country," and it is — until you reach the rock quarry, that is.

Nearing town, you hit a spot where large digging machines and belts are at work all day, carving out the side of an alpine ridge, moving the extracted stone into large piles beside the road. The company has been there for many years and has obviously sold a lot of rock, for hundreds of yards of earth have nearly vanished. The gap looks awkward, as though there's an enormous void in something that was once solid and ought to be beautiful.

The picture is one I return to often. As I look at our world, at my friends and family, at myself, I see and experience a similar kind of void. It feels as though I was once made strong and whole, but something has gone to work on me, hollowing out my insides. It is cliché to say, "I feel empty," when I have done something wrong, but often that is the effect of my failures. Sometimes, thankfully, those places grow back. Sometimes the beauty returns and healing occurs. But sometimes the holes remain. Sometimes healing is elusive and difficult. In fact, sometimes I continue to scrape away more and more of what once made me authentically human.

I am self-centered when I ought to be thoughtful. I hurt those I care for most. Sometimes I'm a coward. Sometimes I'm a fool. Sometimes I give total control of my life to unhealthy appetites that make my life a mess. Recently, a song has been repeating in my head that says over and again, "I don't want to fight. I'm tired of being sorry."[1] They are the words of a broken soul, and I find myself relating all too much.

In my better moments, I ask myself why I am compelled to act in these emptying ways. What is it that inspires such acts? Why can't I simply live out the complete, genuinely robust life I desire to have? It feels as though something is at war with me — within me — that is determined to make my life miserable.

The Bible has a name for this force in us and in our world that is clawing away at what was once solid. It calls the force "sin" and suggests that when early humanity first chose death over life, sin — this active absence — was unleashed and began eroding all that was once good. We ought to think of sin not as human wickedness or immoral actions. Sin is first and foremost a *power*. Augustine wrote that sin "tends to make that which is cease to be."[2] It is a parasitic force, and like all parasites, sin does not exist on its own. It thrives off a host. The unconscious goal of sin — in devils, governments, and ourselves — is to cut pieces out of the fabric of reality and call the incisions "real life."

From the earliest days of Christianity, lists were written naming the manifestations of this power. These lists were not assembled for curiosity's sake. The writers were doing the work of physicians — diagnosing the disease that is killing us. And around the sixth century, one of the lists came to be viewed as definitive. Seven cancers were identified and exposed as the power of sin at work in us, mangling our desires and pointing us toward poisonous delights: *pride* — the natural love for myself magnified and perverted into disdain for others; *envy* — the rejection of the good life God has given me for an obsession with what God gives to someone else; *sloth* — the indifference toward my neighbor, my soul, my world, or my God; *greed* — the desire to possess more than I need because of fear or idolatry; *lust* — the handing of control over my body and mind to illicit cravings; *wrath* — the love for justice perverted into bitterness, revenge, and violence; and *gluttony* — the excessive consumption that deprives another human being of a life-giving necessity. These are the seven expressions of the power of sin at work in our world. These are the seven ways we assault ourselves, those around us, and the world as a whole.

These are the seven deadly sins.

We see these sins parodied in commercials with men passed out on couches after eating Cheetos — as if that's what sloth and gluttony look like. A popular movie featured a religious fanatic killing the "sinners" around him according to their "sins." The list of sins is used to advertise everything from perfumes to cell phones (as though these sins were a desirable stench for our calling plan). There are a lot of bad ideas about the seven deadly sins, but despite the fog, the name is still spot-on. These seven sins are *deadly*, and if they gain a significant hold in our hearts, they will burrow and burrow and burrow until all that was once beautiful in us is torn away like so much sandstone.

Sloth and wrath remold us, taking the image of God and cracking the reflection. We are moved by greed and envy and gluttony to reject the life we were made for. When we say that people are filled with pride or lust, we mean that the power of sin has infected them so thoroughly that their bodies are swarming with these toxins as lungs might swarm with emphysema. These deadly sins are the means by which a world that was created sound and thriving with life is flipped upside down, made to appear as though real happiness could be found by accumulating all one wishes, enjoying every possible pleasure, dominating others, and ultimately serving one's self as the master of all things.

Above all, the deadly sins are a summons into a dead life, a dysfunctional life. And if you are like me, you have received and embraced their invitation countless times. But what you and I really want is freedom. What we want is to break past our addictions and failures. We want the scrapes and claw marks in our souls to heal and our lives to be made whole again.

What we want — above all else — is our own resurrection.

THE SOWER

When Jesus stepped down from the mountain where he had given his greatest teaching, a sick man called out to him.[3] The man's skin was white and blistered, and he had been told for years that he was not allowed to touch anyone. For the sake of his neighbors and friends, the man had lived outside of town. Anytime he entered his village, he had to yell at passersby the words he had come to hate: "Unclean. Unclean." The disease would eventually eat him away, killing his nerves first. Over time, his fingers and feet would disintegrate for lack of feeling. He would find it harder to find food, to do daily chores, to simply survive. The disease ate holes in a body once solid, holes the man hated, holes that stole away all he had.

The man had once been healthy. He had once had a family, but the infection had taken all of it away from him. The infection left him alone. His only future was one in which he would watch his body fall apart. When the man heard about Jesus, he came and threw himself before the miracle worker, begging Jesus to clean the horrid infection from his skin.

When Jesus acted, his touch and blessing were not only a restoration of the leper's flesh; they were an invitation to the man to reenter society, reenter his family circle, and become human again. Jesus' touch filled the voids in this man with life again. The man had been a corpse counting down the last of his pain-ridden days, but Jesus changed that. He took the man's hand, lifted him from his knees, and raised him from the dead.

This is a microcosm of Jesus' work, for nearly every miracle Jesus performed, nearly every word he spoke, was a billboard that read, "God is raising the dead!"

The gospel writers tell us that Jesus' primary activity was traveling "from one town and village to another, proclaiming the good news of the kingdom of God."[4] That is, *Jesus spent his time announcing an event.* Something extraordinary was happening of which Jesus was both herald and instigator. "The time has come," he would say.[5] God was returning to rule a world too long infected with the power of sin. But now God was acting in a new way. He was beginning to set things in order again himself. He was making a dead world Eden once more.

As Jesus walked the roads of Israel, he encouraged everyone he met to give up their agendas and join God in setting all things right. Jesus invited his audience into God's story — the story of the future, the story that would enliven all the earth again, the story in which all things dead would be transformed. Heaven was coming, Jesus said, and it would soon fill every crevice of a world too long eaten away by hell. Jesus' most explicit statement about God's future came in the story often called "the parable of the sower":

> "A farmer went out to sow his seed. As he was scattering the seed, some fell along the path; it was trampled on, and the birds ate it up. Some fell on rock, and when it came up, the plants withered because they had no moisture. Other seed fell among thorns, which grew up with it and choked the plants. Still other seed fell on good soil. It came up and yielded a crop, a hundred times more than was sown."
>
> When he said this, he called out, "Whoever has ears to hear, let them hear."[6]

This was the first parable Jesus told, and it is the most important.[7]

After telling this parable, Jesus said, "If you can't understand the meaning of this parable, how will you understand all the other parables?"[8] Jesus never again said anything like this. *He intentionally drew his listeners' attention to this unique spot.* Jesus offered this parable as the primary clue for understanding everything else he would say and do. It is the key to understanding all of Christ's work.

On the face of things, the parable doesn't seem too important. We get it. Good soil versus bad soil. Change your heart. We've heard the Sunday school songs. It's fairly elementary. But notice, when Jesus finished the story, *he called out* to the crowd, "Whoever has ears to hear, let them hear."[9] This was a passionate invitation to go deeper, as though he were saying, "Everyone, listen! There's more to this parable than you think."[10] He was, in fact, offering an explicit invitation to his followers to pull the story apart and look closer. So let's consider the symbols here.

First, what is going on with this farmer, and why is he so reckless with his seed? Jesus seems to be telling a story in which the farmer is deliberately wasteful, scattering seed everywhere, even on the path beneath his own feet. Why would the farmer spread seed *everywhere*? This doesn't seem to be a good gardening practice. Rather, it seems as though the farmer is being intentionally gracious to even the worst kind of soil.

Next, consider the location. Where is this farmer throwing his seeds? This is probably happening in a field or garden — a place where you grow stuff — and this is a significant clue. Anytime Jesus mentions a "garden," he is directing our attention back to Eden — and Eden is about how things ought to be. But notice, in *this* garden there are weeds, thorns, soil wearing Kevlar, and nasty, seed-eating birds. This garden has gone downhill. Anti-seed, anti-crop forces have infiltrated the farmer's field and are eager to stop anything from growing there.

Now some may suggest that if the farmer in the story was good, wise, and powerful, he would simply kill the birds, destroy the weeds, and tear out the rocky soil — right?[11] Isn't that the obvious course of action? Possibly, but it seems this farmer knows something we don't. *He knows the quality of the seed in his pockets.* He knows that killing birds and ripping up the earth are unnecessary, for once this seed finds root in the ground, its power will be overwhelming. When the seed takes root, it will affect everything else. And as Jesus closed his parable, we see just that. This seemingly wasteful farmer, Jesus said, received back "a crop, a hundred times more than was sown."[12] This by all accounts would have filled the entire garden with the crop, pushing it to capacity. All the space that was once empty and barren would have been jammed with the fruit the farmer chose to bear. It's a miracle, and it displays precisely the work Jesus would accomplish on earth.

The picture Jesus painted for his audience — the picture that should color everything we think about Jesus' life, death, and resurrection — is the fruit filling every emptiness in a world that was made to be Eden but is barren and lifeless.

Jesus revisited this image in many of his other stories. In the parable of the tenants, a landowner plants a vineyard in order to bear fruit, but the tenants produce nothing for him. So the landowner takes the vineyard and gives it to others, *because the fruit* — not the tenant — *is what matters.*[13] In a story called the parable of the workers in the vineyard, a landowner hires laborers all day long — even until the last hour — and pays everyone a full day's wage to come and bear fruit in his garden. The landowner is reckless with his cash, *because he thinks the fruit* — not the wage — *is what matters.*[14] In another parable, a tree has been growing without fruit in a man's field for three years, and the owner decides to give it one more year to yield a harvest, but after that he will cut it down. It may have been a lovely tree, but the man calls it worthless, *because the fruit* — not the tree — *is what matters.*[15]

When the disciples later asked Jesus what the parable of the sower meant, he gave them still more clues:

"The knowledge of the secrets of the kingdom of God has been given to you, but to others I speak in parables, so that,

"'though seeing, they may not see;
  though hearing, they may not understand.'

"This is the meaning of the parable: The seed is the word of God. Those along the path are the ones who hear, and then the devil comes and takes away the word from their hearts, so that they may not believe and be saved. Those on the rock are the ones who receive the word with joy when they hear it, but they have no root. They believe for a while, but in the time of testing they fall away. The seed that fell among thorns stands for those who hear, but as they go on their way they are choked by life's worries, riches and pleasures, and they do not mature. But the seed on good soil stands for those with a noble and good heart, who hear the word, retain it, and by persevering produce a crop."[16]

In one sense there is a clear message here: Be like the soil that received the word of God with a good heart. However, it is obvious that Jesus thinks this parable is explosive. Why would he need to say after the first telling, "Whoever has ears, let them hear," if all the parable meant was, "Be good and bear fruit"? Why say, "I speak in parables so they may not see, so they may not understand"? Telling people around you, "Just have a good heart, man," simply isn't that controversial. So what is it that's so revolutionary here?

The key to understanding this parable is not the question, *what* is the seed? but *who* is the seed? And Jesus told us. The seed is the Word of God. And the Word of God, we might note, is Jesus.[17] Jesus is the seed the farmer is planting everywhere, the seed whose crop will consume the entire garden. Jesus — his life and healing and rule — is the seed that will renovate every square inch of our world, our relationships, and ourselves.

This parable is an announcement of a worldwide revolution in which evil, sin, and death are not purged but totally overrun, as though they were merely empty space needing to be filled again.

Jesus believed that God's restorative power was overwhelming the holes dug not only in the world's power structures but in lost humanity itself. Neither the tyrants who controlled his country nor the religious elite who would later kill him nor the pagan gods happy with barren fields nor the darkened human heart within us all, Jesus said, can withstand the restorative power of God's Word filling in every void, everywhere. As biblical scholar E. P. Sanders wrote, "Jesus did not expect the end of the world in the sense of destruction of the cosmos. He expected a divine, transforming miracle."[18]

Jesus referred to God's restorative rule breaking into a void-filled earth as "the kingdom of heaven." For Jesus, heaven is not something we wait for. Heaven is something to be embraced and spread now. Jesus taught his followers to pray, "Your will be done, on earth as it is in heaven."[19] And Jesus believed that was precisely what was beginning to happen. God's restorative rule was beginning to put back together all that had been slashed and burned by the power of sin. It was an event to be welcomed. It was an event to celebrate.

This more than anything else was the good news that Jesus announced as he went from town to town. This is the gospel, and this gospel is all about resurrection.

A NEW WAY TO BE HUMAN

As a little kid, I remember watching my first movie about God.[20] I had never seen God before — on the screen or in real life — so this was important information for an irreligious eight-year-old. In the movie, God dressed like an elderly man from Missouri. He wore a sky-blue button-up shirt tucked into beige pants placed a little too high on his hips. He pulled a goofy white hat down low near his eyebrows, and he was old. Very old. This God would have looked right at home in a Las Vegas casino, and, in fact, that was where the movie was shot. God walked past multicolored lights and slot machines, and he took a seat at a lonely poker table next to a man who had the exact same face.

Though they looked like twins, the other man wasn't into retirement home fashion. He wore an expensive black suit with a red tie. His eyes weren't filled with wisdom or welcome, like God's were. His were eyes of distrust. Watching the movie, you didn't need to ask who the man in the black suit was. He welcomed God, the two began catching up, and then God asked about a specific soul on whom the black-suited man had a unique claim. The man in black acknowledged the soul while the dealer shuffled a deck before them. And as God and the Devil spoke, they began playing cards.

This was the climax of the film. The two battled for the soul of some unfortunate guy, and their weapons were poker cards. It was an interesting twist, but everyone watching knew who would win. God could change his pair of threes into four aces. God could overwhelm the fear glands in the Devil's brain so he would immediately fold and run out of the room screaming. God could turn back time over and over again until his hand was just perfect.

That whole "all-powerful" thing can be a real advantage when playing cards.

But the movie didn't hinge on the cards being played. In fact, as the hands are dealt, we don't pay attention to them. *What we care about is the dialogue.* We want to know what evil will say to goodness, and what goodness will say in return. That's where the action is. It will not do for God to walk up to the poker table like Clint Eastwood, draw a lightning bolt from his holster, and send evil sprawling to the floor. God cannot win the day like that. We must hear something else.

As they speak, we need to see the lifestyle of heaven as superior to that of hell. The good life must not only be good; it must also be the happy life, the wonder-filled life, the attractively complete life. It must be, in fact, the best life worth living. So too, God must show that a hellish lifestyle isn't merely undesirable. It is pathetic and falling apart. He must show that the hell-ridden life is one that begins in decay and ends in decay, and only the pitiable embrace it.

Nothing less will do.

When we watch films depicting the struggle between good and evil, we need good to overcome evil — not with power, not with tricks, not with lucky flukes, but through its goodness. Only then will *we* have a reason to walk the hard roads where goodness often leads us. Such confrontations give us hope that, yes, the sacrifices we make, the passions we restrain, the drops of blood we give are not vanity but are marks of the complete and happy life.

In such moments, we need God to speak, because soon we will leave the theater. Soon we will turn off our television or close our book, and we will enter our normal rhythms again. We will begin to make hard decisions about what we want and how we will treat others. And when we begin to ask tough questions about our lifestyle, we will need something worth saying to our own devils when they inevitably come chomping. This is the duel at hand. The battle between heaven and hell is waged with bold invitations, and the soul hanging in the balance is not some unfortunate fictional character.

The soul being played for is our own.

When Jesus began to announce that heaven was engulfing our world, he had to do more than show this reality through miracles. He had to show that God's work was *desirable*. He had to awaken the passions of his audience so they would devote themselves fully to the difficult work God was doing all around them. In his own words, he had to convince them that God's work was worth giving away one's entire life for,[21] like a man selling everything he had to buy land with a wondrous treasure buried within.[22]

As Jesus entered the synagogues of northern Israel and spoke from its streets and hillsides, he used the same phrase over and over again to excite his listeners and invite their devotion: "Repent, for the kingdom of heaven has come near."[23]

Now if you and I went out in the streets of our towns or onto the campus of a local university and said with a loud voice, "Repent, for the kingdom of heaven has come near," those listening would hear something like, "Give up your private sins! Get religion! The end of the world is coming! I am a crazy person!" But those in Jesus' day would have heard something much different. It would have sounded more like, "Stop. Give up your personal agenda and come join me. God is starting an uprising. He's returning to set everything right again."[24]

Of course, any fool can claim to be God's messenger, but because of Jesus' miraculous power, word spread everywhere concerning him. People walked dozens of miles to hear him speak. Monstrous crowds assembled everywhere he went, and each time Jesus held the attention of his audience, he would sit down and give a sermon.

The same sermon.

Luke records the time when Jesus gave this sermon on a desert plain. In Matthew's gospel, Jesus delivered it from a mountainside. We call the content of this teaching "the Sermon on the Mount," and for the first year of his public life, this was how Jesus introduced himself and invited his audience to choose the life of heaven.[25] Through this sermon, Jesus told his audience how God saw things, what God was doing, and what God cared about most. It was much different from what anyone expected.

We often read passages from the Sermon on the Mount — passages about not lusting or not hating others, about going the extra mile, loving our enemies, not judging another, turning the other cheek, bearing fruit with our lives — as good advice or good rules to follow.

But that is not what is going on here. Throughout this sermon, Jesus described a new way to be human.

The sermon began with what ancient writers have called "the Beatitudes." The Beatitudes are eight snapshots of eight different lives that Jesus said experience God's favor.[26] The Beatitudes introduced all that Jesus wanted to say about a new kind of life. Through them Jesus sought to pull at his audience's heartstrings. He wanted to draw them in and show them that the life God offers is precisely what they desired. The Beatitudes were, above all else, Jesus' invitation to see the world as God does — and to love it.

As a whole, *the Beatitudes are a picture of the voids created by sin being filled in with the life of heaven.* They are eight pictures of resurrection.

The first four beatitudes focus on the poor, meek, mourning, and thirsty — all people we consider wretched. But more than anything, the poor in spirit, the mourning and meek, those thirsting for righteousness *would have seen themselves as rejected by God.* Everything in their culture would have screamed out that these people were unworthy of God's love and affection, that their lives would remain miserable, that they were as good as dead. Jesus spoke directly to these people and raised their chins:

Blessed are the poor in spirit — those who know they lack what makes them alive and who look to others for help — *for theirs is the kingdom of heaven.*

Blessed are those who mourn — those who have had that which they care for most stripped away — *for they will be comforted.*

Blessed are the meek — those who do not pursue power or authority but live gentle lives in my kingdom — *for they will inherit the earth.*

Blessed are those who hunger and thirst for righteousness — those who have no good thing inside themselves yet still long for something real — *for they will be filled.*[27]

This was good news. Many of those listening had been told or knew implicitly that their misery was the result of their own deviation from God. They had been taught that power and physical glory characterized the happy life. But Jesus — this preacher exercising God's power over every disease and demon he encountered — told them that comfort, inheritance, wholeness, and heaven were theirs *where they were.*[28] That though they saw themselves as dead, God saw them as alive.

The last four beatitudes commend the merciful, the peacemakers, the pure in heart, and the persecuted. Often it is these who strive for goodness with no apparent reward. It is these who — though bent low for God — receive nothing but sorrow for their self-giving. And Jesus said to them, "In my kingdom, under my rule, you will be shown mercy. You will see God. You will be called children of God. You will be like the prophets, receiving their same reward, their same blessing, their same measure of happiness."

Again, this is a picture of the world being restored. The holes are being filled in. Jesus removed his listeners from the noise and trash that the cultures around them offered, and instead praised a different kind of praiseworthiness:

Blessed are the merciful — those who give even out of their
    want — *for they will be shown mercy.*

Blessed are the pure in heart — those whose insides are dedicated
    to what actually matters — *for they will see God.*

Blessed are the peacemakers — who work for the same ends
    I do — *for they [too] will be called children of God.*

Blessed are those who are persecuted because of righteousness — who live the life of God in broken places, showcasing God's reign — *for theirs is the kingdom of heaven.*[29]

These beatitudes are cheers from the farmer to those who work the soil in his garden. They are encouragement to those who feel as though their life is a constant battle with no apparent victories. They are a message of hope to those who anticipate a day when the holes in our world are finally filled and everything is made new.

Thus the Beatitudes are one part invitation and one part acclimation. The Beatitudes are some of the sights we see when heaven and earth overlap and interlock. More than anything, they are Jesus' appeal to the brokenhearted and the arrogant, the virtuous and the self-assured, to awaken, to turn their perspective right side up and not only see the world as God does, but desire it.

And at their core, the Beatitudes are Jesus' portrait of a dead world resurrected from the clutches of the seven deadly sins.

Two Invitations

When our oldest son was born, a good friend of ours got him a short-sleeved black Onesie with red trim. It has a picture of Darth Vader's mask on the front, and underneath it in bold red letters, it reads, "WHO'S YOUR DADDY?" It makes me laugh, but of course it refers to a sinister event. This is the temptation of Luke Skywalker to turn his heart and mind over to the dark side.

From the outset of the original Star Wars trilogy, we see that Darth Vader stands for evil; Obi-Wan Kenobi represents goodness; and there's a struggle for the heart of Luke Skywalker and his future. Each time good and evil speak to Skywalker, they invite him to see the world as they do — telling him what is valuable, what is worthy of his pursuit, where real life is found. Kenobi and Vader each speak in invitations: Come into this kind of life, this kind of reality; be transformed; follow me; this is who you are made to be; this is your destiny.

So too the Beatitudes; so too the seven deadly sins.

The Beatitudes and the deadly sins are two sets of invitations. Looking at them in turn, we see two paths available to us. Both call to deep places within us to come and taste. Both present themselves as life as it actually is. Both invite us to take up residence. But only one will make us happy, for one is life, full and awake; the other is the absence, the nothingness. In the Beatitudes and the deadly sins, we see heaven and hell and we hear the words they speak to us.

Perhaps you're like me, and when you see the list of deadly sins — envy and lust, wrath and greed, sloth, pride, and gluttony — they are not like a foreign language that you can speak but generally avoid. For me, the deadly sins describe how I normally think, what I normally want, and how I normally behave. The seven deadly sins illustrate my everyday rhythms. They are often the unconscious guide I follow.

And they just don't seem to work anymore.

I want something else. I desire someone to fill these empty places in me, but often I don't know what will do the job. Yes, I've loved God for a long time and pray for his help and guidance, for the strength to change. But often the holes just feel too deep. At times I feel like I don't have the energy to wrestle anymore. It's easier to give myself over to these tendencies, to these voids — to just let them do their thing.

But yet another part of me says this just isn't right. This is not how things are supposed to be. I want to be alive in ways I can only dream of. I want to shed this deadweight and run again. I want what I think Jesus had. Passion. Joy. Wonder. An invigorated soul.

The Beatitudes offer me — and offer you — that reality. They are the antidote to the poisons we so readily consume. If only we could see where they speak to the infected places inside us, allow them to push back the void, and watch as they regrow our humanity. If only Jesus' words would speak directly to the deadly sins in your life and mine, perhaps then we would know what happiness is. Perhaps then we could truly say, "This is what I was made for. This is who I was meant to be. This is heaven." Perhaps then we would see the road leading clearly toward our own resurrection.

1

PRIDE AND
THE POOR IN SPIRIT

One is the loneliest number.
THREE DOG NIGHT

THE STORY IS TOLD OF A MAN WHO HAD A DREAM IN WHICH AN ANGEL showed him two doors — one marked Heaven and the other Hell.[1] Curious, the man went to the door marked Hell. Inside he saw an unhappy sight. Twelve emaciated people sat around a cauldron of steaming hot soup. Beside them were large spoons — too large, in fact. The spoons required both arms and all one's might to lift and place in the cauldron. Many were able to get food on the end, but the weight of the spoons caused them to tip over as the people brought the food to their lips. Those in hell were never able to eat from the deep cauldrons. The spoons were too long, too heavy.

"Most in hell," the angel explained, "have spent long hours trying to feed themselves but have failed again and again."

The dreamer watched them staring, starving, and he recoiled from hell's doorway. *These people have no hope*, he thought. It seemed that God was mocking them. "It is torture," he said to the angel, "to have what you desire sitting before you yet be unable to have even a taste!"

Turning, he opened the door marked Heaven. Inside he saw

twelve people sitting around a deep cauldron of soup, with spoons too large to lift to their lips. The room was the same as the one in hell — the same light, the same size — but in this room there was a joy unlike anything the man had ever seen. He and the angel were caught up in the laughter. There was even singing, and the people celebrated for long hours as the soup sat boiling before them.

Leaving, the man was puzzled by the contrast between the two rooms. One so filled with joy and the other a prison of misery. Certainly those in heaven were in denial. Perhaps they had grown content with want. Looking at the angel, the dreamer asked why those in heaven were happy while those in hell were not.

"Those in heaven have learned to feed each other," said the angel.

Whereas the kingdom of heaven is communal and bent toward the service of others, the attitude of hell assumes everything exists for me — to serve me, benefit me — because I am that significant.

John Milton's classic *Paradise Lost* begins with Satan falling from the presence of God into a dark world. Looking around, he affirms himself by saying, "Better to reign in Hell, than serve in Heav'n."[2] Some move toward the void of hell — not because reality is too ugly or painful, but because the kingdom of heaven is about others and not one's self. And when all people everywhere stop serving one another and begin groping for what is "rightfully theirs," this inward focus becomes deadly. The ancients called this attitude of persistent self-focus *pride*, and when pride takes hold of a culture, everyone starves.

Pride is the natural love for myself magnified and perverted into disdain for others. Augustine called pride the foundation of sin, for "pride made the soul desert God, to whom it should cling as the source of life, and to imagine itself instead as the source of its own life."[3] In other words, the more I make my life, my well-being, my enlightenment, and my success primary, the farther I step from reality. Thus the hell-bound do not travel downward; they travel inward, cocooning themselves behind a mass of vanity, personal rights, religiosity, and defensiveness.

Obsession with self is the defining mark of a disintegrating soul. Unlike the other sins, pride usually appears when I am at my best. Pride capitalizes not just on my failures but even more so on my successes. When I choose to abstain from base desires, gluttony and lust may be defeated, but not pride. Pride tells me what a fine person I am for resisting such rubbish — and my eyes turn inward. When I fast, pride is there to pat me on the back and tell me what a devout person I am — and again my eyes turn inward. If I stop fasting so I won't draw attention to myself, pride marks the occasion with trumpets. If I share wisdom or withhold it, if I give money or refrain, if I pray or remain silent — pride is always there as a false light to bask in. No matter what I do, pride loves to hold up my reflection as an idol to be cherished.

We're each capable of turning what we see in the mirror into our god. I see this tendency clearly in myself when I believe I have all the right answers, not just for me but for those I judge as having messed-up lives and messed-up beliefs. "If they only knew what I know, their lives would be so much better," I say to myself. I am comfortable with such condescension because in the back of my mind, I think God agrees with my opinion. (And he has clout.) I'm just offering clear-headed discernment because I am that close to the divine.

Smells rotten, huh?

One writer said that pride is the only sickness that makes everyone ill except the one who has it.[4] We ought to take this a step further, because pride hurts everyone, *especially* the proud. Those in the vicinity of pride may be stepped on, abused, dismissed, even shot in order to keep the pristine image of the proud intact. But self-obsession ultimately destroys the proud soul. It eliminates every life-giving relationship the proud may have enjoyed. Even God draws close to the proud,[5] but the proud cannot draw close to God or anyone else, for *pride destroys our ability to connect with others*. Perhaps this is why many great Christian thinkers have identified pride as the first lethal step into hell's hands.[6] Pride chooses itself over the rest of reality. It is the complete antirealist frame of mind.

Pride, then, is not possessing extraordinary talents, viewing my skills highly, or even showcasing my gifts for the benefit of others. Pride instead spurs me to view myself as the *only* one in the entire world who matters, to think that I have somehow earned the prime spot in the universe, and now all of creation is a grand symphony celebrating me. I may have a lowly job, no money, no friends, no iPhone, yet still meditate continually on myself as the one whose thoughts and feelings matter more than anyone else's.

Pride is not thinking too much of myself; pride is thinking of myself far too much.

Jesus told a story of a man with two sons, both consumed with themselves.[7] The younger brother's pride led him to waste everything he had been given — his identity, his inheritance, his past. His conceit ultimately led him into the isolation of a foreign land. When his poverty became too much for him to bear, he thought of the riches back home and returned to his father, hoping to become a hired hand. His father would not have it. He welcomed his boy back as his son and threw a mighty celebration.

The older brother, seeing his father's reckless pity on the younger son, also left his father's home. He had never been given a party. He had never had a calf butchered in his honor, so he left his father's house. The older son was proud, and just like his younger brother, hubris led the older son into isolation. When the father came to him to draw him back into his family, the older son recited a long list of accomplishments to his father — his obedience, his steadfast resolve. His statements proved not that he wanted to be a son, but that he, like his younger brother, longed to be just another hired hand.

Because of their self-infatuation, both sons moved from the company of their family into seclusion. When the father went out to his sons, each told the father of his desire to work and earn his status, and this made them *less* sonlike. Of course, the father in Jesus' story didn't need another hired hand. The father wanted children who would stand beside him by his fence and look out for runaways, who would celebrate when it was time to celebrate, who would live and love as he did. In his words to both sons, the father invited them to become more like him — clothed in his splendor, given his authority, and celebrating the rich life they have together. Yet in their pride, both boys demanded life on their own terms. They wanted to step away from the reality their father had fashioned. They wanted to create a kingdom for themselves rather than a kingdom with others.

Pride always leads us into isolation, for one cannot love when one is alone. A loveless life is a hellish life. Jesus often characterized hell as the darkness outside, as a place of solitude. And solitude is the opposite of the kingdom of heaven.

A VAST CHASM

Jesus once told a story of two men who died and were taken to a different world. One was a wealthy man who dressed in the comforts of royalty and lived in luxury every day. At his gate was a beggar named Lazarus. Sores covered Lazarus's body, and his only companions were the dogs who came to lick his wounds. One man served himself exclusively; he even had large walls to keep out the desperate. The other man, even in his poverty, allowed the hungry to feed on his own flesh.[8] Jesus picks up the story after the two men died:

> "The time came when the beggar died and the angels carried him to Abraham's side. The rich man also died and was buried. In Hades,[9] where he was in torment, he looked up and saw Abraham far away, with Lazarus by his side. So he called to him, 'Father Abraham, have pity on me and send Lazarus to dip the tip of his finger in water and cool my tongue, because I am in agony in this fire.'
>
> "But Abraham replied, 'Son, remember that in your lifetime you received your good things, while Lazarus received bad things, but now he is comforted here and you are in agony. And besides all this, between us and you a great chasm has been set in place, so that those who want to go from here to you cannot, nor can anyone cross over from there to us.'
>
> "He answered, 'Then I beg you, father, send Lazarus to my family, for I have five brothers. Let him warn them, so that they will not also come to this place of torment.'
>
> "Abraham replied, 'They have Moses and the Prophets; let them listen to them.'
>
> "'No, father Abraham,' he said, 'but if someone from the dead goes to them, they will repent.'
>
> "He said to him, 'If they do not listen to Moses and the Prophets, they will not be convinced even if someone rises from the dead.'"[10]

As he does with pictures of camels bounding through the eye of a needle, large boards sticking from a woman's eye, and grown men being born again, Jesus paints a surreal picture with this story so we might see something far more significant than a point-by-point tour of the afterlife.[11]

In this story, a large chasm separates the rich man from Lazarus, who was taken to "Abraham's side." In the Jewish world, this was a reference to feasting.[12] If you and I had gone to a party in Jesus' day, we would not have sat in chairs; we would have sat on the floor at a low table, and to avoid falling over, we might have leaned against one another's sides.[13] Here at Abraham's side, Lazarus is no longer in the company of dogs. Instead, he is in the intimate presence of his great ancestor.

In contrast, the rich man is in an unbearable situation. He is on fire yet somehow is not burning up, and there is a canyon that keeps him isolated and alone. To converse with anyone, he must yell across a wide, empty chasm.

Then something happens. The rich man — on fire and alone — begins speaking to Abraham, making requests of Lazarus to do things for him — get him water, send a message on his behalf. The rich man believes he still has some standing. He thinks he can command the beggar who used to sit at his gates. The rich man does not believe Lazarus is his equal; he thinks Lazarus is an inferior to be sent on such menial errands as fetching water.

When the rich man doesn't get his way, he begins to argue with Abraham — which any devout Jew of that day would recognize as an act of unbelievable arrogance, one approaching blasphemy. But the rich man — alone, dead, and on fire — still thinks he has clout. The rich man still thinks he's special because he used to dress in purple and could afford large gates. His present condition is not enough of a neon sign to alert him to the fact that his earthly life was a failure and his present condition is the result.

Of course, it did not take the rich man's dying for him to be placed on the wrong side of a chasm. He built that chasm through self-obsession. He didn't have to die for his soul to catch fire. Flaming pride consumed the man well before his death. The rich man's pride led to his solitude. His arrogance created the canyon widening before him. The hell Jesus described in this parable is not so much a future condition. Hell was for this man the story of his lonesome, flame-ridden life. He used his power not to help others but to build bigger walls to keep them out. He used his money not to cover the sores of a desperate man but to cover himself with fine clothes. And as in life, in death he has no one to lean against.

What would have happened if the rich man had served Lazarus and healed his sores? What would have happened if he had ripped down the gate separating them and stooped low to help the beggar? What would have happened if he had served Lazarus with the gifts he had been given?

The rich man would have entered into a relationship with Lazarus. He would have allowed Lazarus to lean on him for provision. In a profound way, the rich man would have assumed the role that Jesus reserved for one of the great men of Israel's past. *The rich man would have found himself in the place of Abraham with Lazarus the beggar at his side.* It is this kind of interdependence that matters to God, and this is rightly seen as the life of heaven.

An Everlasting Community

"I love it when you fail."

"You and I will never be friends."

"My cell phone is smaller than yours."

A recent video by the band Seether shows all sorts of people looking at us, their mouths closed but their hands holding signs with messages like these:

"I am a product of sex and violence."

"I disgust myself."

"I used to believe."

"I'm boring in bed."

"I am a liar."

"I slept with 432 women."

"I have shallow, unrealistic dreams."[14]

The sign holders stare at the camera with lonely eyes, as though the repressed messages there on paper are cutting away their insides. Just as a small dose of poison will kill a rat because rodents cannot vomit, so too a small toxic belief will kill a human soul. Those who deal with their problems alone, it seems, are easily destroyed by them.

Recently, I watched an episode of *The Simpsons* that parodied a bad horror film. Desperate and on the run from an *I Know What You Did Last Summer* Ned Flanders, Homer says to his family, "OK, Marge, you hide in the abandoned amusement park; Lisa, the pet cemetery; Bart, spooky roller disco; and I'll go skinny-dipping in that lake where the sexy teens were killed a hundred years ago tonight."[15] And that's how horror films work: divide and conquer. When people are split up, they lose their power. The directors of these films love to separate their characters because those who are alone are easily destroyed.

We instinctively know this to be true. Imagine being forced to camp in a dark wilderness. The trees around you cast long shadows. You have to get water by yourself, you have to get firewood by yourself, and at some point you will have to go to sleep. Many of us feel uneasy just at the thought of it.

Now imagine you are in the exact same place with five friends.

For most of us, the feeling totally changes. Our fear evaporates. The night outdoors may even be fun. Yet when we are alone, we are thrown into survival mode, because when we are alone, we have no power. When we are alone, we are vulnerable to anything that might attack us. When we are alone, we are easily destroyed.

A few months ago I went on a retreat with sixty or so people. On the second day, the leader got out his pen and wrote down this formula: Privacy + Time = Destruction.

There is a reason those with toxic beliefs and no one to speak to are dying inside. There is a reason horror films split up the hormone-crazed eighteen-year-olds when it's time to let the monsters out. There is a reason you and I would feel terrified if left in the woods by ourselves: Privacy + Time = Destruction.

The idea is part of our deep subconscious. If we are alone, it is only a matter of time before we'll be snuffed out.[16] There's a simple explanation for why we feel this way: *We were not made to be alone.*

In Genesis 1, as God creates stars and land masses, oceans and ecosystems, he looks at the things he has made and, over and again, thinks to himself, "It is good. It is good. It is good."[17] Then in Genesis 2, he creates a man, the crown jewel of his entire creation. This should be the culminating moment. God has placed in his beautiful world the one who was meant to become his son. But here God stops. He pauses. And for the very first time, when God speaks, he does not create something new. His words, in fact, have a hint of melancholy. Looking on the man who shares his breath, God says, "It is not good for the man to be alone."[18]

It seems the entire creation was no longer good because a *solitary* man stood at its center.

God heals the loneliness by creating out of the man "a helper,"[19] and her entrance affects the entire created order. The life of Adam is given to Eve. The life of Eve is made to be given to Adam. Two persons are born through and for each other; and the two, says God, "will become one flesh."[20] With this new activity at the center of his new world, God's entire opinion of the cosmos shifts. Now when God looks on his work, it has a new beauty, for at the core of creation are now self-surrender and unity. Now when "God saw all that he had made," the creation had reached a new status; now "it was *very good*."[21]

Self-giving community changed everything.

Because of its goodness, even God entered creation. In Genesis 3, he is "walking in the garden in the cool of the day."[22] The word here for "cool" is *rûah*, which is the primary Hebrew word for God's Spirit.[23] So the initial picture of creation — in which human beings are giving all for one another — has the Spirit of God filling the whole world, becoming its very atmosphere. Everything is whole. It's as though heaven and earth overlap, as though the kingdom of heaven is at hand.

When Jesus spoke, his favorite topic was not love. It was not peace. It was not grace. Though all of these were important to him, Jesus' favorite topic — the subject at the heart of every story he told and every miracle he performed — was the kingdom of heaven.

Jesus taught us to pray, "Our Father in heaven, . . . your kingdom come, . . . on earth as it is in heaven."[24] He consistently painted pictures for his disciples that would start with the phrase "The kingdom of heaven is like . . .": The kingdom of heaven is like a wedding feast that none of the posh attended, so the Father threw open the doors and invited everyone everywhere to fill his banquet halls.[25] The kingdom of heaven is like a king who forgave all those who owed him unpayable debts and then asked the forgiven to forgive in the same way.[26] The kingdom of heaven is like a lost son who in his desperation remembered his father's house and returned to find his father waiting for him, ready to throw a mighty celebration.[27]

For Jesus, the kingdom of heaven is always about people coming together.

You and I know this intuitively. Often we experience heaven when we are with our closest friends. We can sit over a meal for hours and think, "This is what I was made for. This is what life is supposed to be like." It's because we were made for the tribe, made for the pack, made for the circle of friends.

Jesus gave moral teachings that encouraged his followers to become the type of people who naturally care for the good of others because he wanted them to be united as a family. The life of heaven focuses on the good of others. It picks up the spoon not to fill its own belly but to offer a bite to the other starving stomachs in the room. This is the best life possible because it is the very type of life that is going on within God. The Father gives us his Son.[28] The Son gives us his life.[29] The Spirit gives us understanding of all that is true and praiseworthy.[30] *This* reckless self-giving is the activity of heaven. Jesus said that all God wishes for you and me — all he encourages us to do and be, the entirety of our moral obligation — is summed up in this kind of reckless self-giving toward God and others.[31] As we are drawn to one another, we experience the life of heaven. As in the story of Lazarus, heaven is life together, where one can lean against someone and be able to eat; conversely, hell is life alone, where one must shout in order to be heard.

Running on Empty

There's a long stretch of highway between Las Vegas and the California border with only desert on each side. A few years ago, my brother Wes and I became quite familiar with this patch of road, because somewhere in the dead center, we ran out of gas. It took a few hours of enduring the 110-degree heat to find a gas station, fill up a gas can, and return to our car, walking along the black Nevada pavement. It would have truly made us happy to have known twenty miles earlier that we were running out of gas. Our belief that we were full and fully capable made for a long, miserable summer afternoon.

Sometimes knowing you're empty isn't a curse. Sometimes it's a blessing.

The Beatitudes start precisely here. Jesus did not begin the invitation to his audience with a message to "fill up." Instead, Jesus affirmed those who were empty in the most significant way imaginable: "Blessed are the poor in spirit, for theirs is the kingdom of heaven."[32] This was not an encouragement to *become* poor in spirit; it was addressed to those who were poor in spirit already, elevating them to the highest status possible.

Eugene Petersen translates Matthew 5:3, "You're blessed when you're at the end of your rope."[33] Dallas Willard interprets it, "Blessed are the spiritual zeros — the spiritually bankrupt, deprived and deficient, the spiritual beggars, those without a wisp of 'religion.'"[34] Robyn Griffith-Jones renders it, "Blessed are those who know themselves poor."[35] A popular study Bible puts it this way: "[Blessed are] 'the poverty-stricken in spiritual things' — the simpleminded, the untalented, the religiously unsophisticated."[36] The bottom line is this: Being *"poor in spirit" is a condition, not a prescription.*[37] Being spiritually poor is something you are, not something you seek to become.

When God first created Adam out of the dust, God breathed into his nostrils the breath — the *rûaḥ* — of life, and the man became a living being.[38] As we saw before, *rûaḥ* is the Hebrew word for "spirit." This spirit makes us alive. This spirit sustains us and makes us more than mere dust. When the spirit leaves us, we become dust again. So those poor in spirit are dying; they are lacking the life that was once breathed into their lungs. Jesus' blessing on the poor in spirit is a blessing on those who have lost much of the breath that God first gave them. They are lacking what once made them alive.

So when Jesus spoke of the poor in spirit, who was he referring to? Who is this misfortunate bunch in such desperate need?

Everyone.

All of us have places that are filled not with the spirit of God but with the void of sin. Everyone has broken and disgusting spots in their lives that just won't heal right. Everyone fails. Everyone hurts those they love most. Everyone lacks the kindness, the courage, and the wisdom they ought to possess. No one is solid inside; everyone is deficient.

Jesus alone shows us that our condition is not hopeless. Just as Socrates knew that the only ones who are wise are those who *know* they are fools,[39] so too Jesus shows us that the only ones who are complete are those who *know* they are falling apart. Heaven is occupied not by those who think they have it all together. Heaven is the refuge of the infirm and the mending.

"Blessed are the poor in spirit, for theirs is the kingdom of heaven."

Being poor in spirit is like being part of an AA meeting where all the participants confess openly that their lives have become unmanageable. Poverty in spirit is a conversation over coffee in which tears and regrets and inadequacies cover the table. Poverty in spirit is no longer keeping the toxic things bottled up within — or merely written on signs that read, "I disgust myself," or "I have shallow, unrealistic dreams." It is ripping the tape from my mouth and confessing that I am in desperate need, that things inside me are tragically out of order and I lack the life I ought to have. Those who know they are poor in spirit are blessed because *they alone know they need help* — and any step toward help must be a step toward community.

Jesus said to those who acknowledge their spiritual poverty that "theirs is the kingdom of heaven," because here in heaven we thrive on codependency. Here in heaven we suffer and mend together. Here in heaven the language we speak assumes that you and I are one, that we need each other, that healing comes when we exhale all the toxic things within us by confessing them. Total exposure is not a requirement to enjoy heaven; total exposure is what enjoying heaven looks like.

When we make our hurts and our past and our junk public, we are healed. When we keep them private, it is only a matter of time before they destroy us. Every story about a fall from grace is first a story about privacy. Every story about dramatic restoration of character is first a story of exposure. When Adam and Eve failed, they ran for fig leaves. When Jesus was crucified, he was unclothed. The life of heaven despises fig leaves, for it longs to breathe honest air — even if it means taking up a cross and hanging naked from it.

And yet one vice above all others begs us to avoid exposure, to hold our chin up and pretend instead. Pride vigorously guards the chain binding us to solitude. Pride loves the masks that hide our lonesome faces. Pride insists that we are just fine and tells us that no one will respect us if we expose the places we've failed. Pride prefers isolation to the kingdom of heaven.

Because pride stands as the most significant barrier to kingdom life, God targets it first in the pursuit of the fully healed and restored life.[40] The execution of our pride is essential to our drawing close to God and others. Therefore, God may remove our pride through drastic means — pain, failure, even through the other six deadly sins.[41] The great theologian Thomas Aquinas once wrote:

> In order to overcome their pride, God punishes certain men by allowing them to fall into sins of the flesh, which though they be less grievous are more evidently shameful.... From this indeed the gravity of pride is made manifest. For just as a wise physician, in order to cure a worse disease, *allows* the patient to contract one that is less dangerous, so the sin of pride is shown to be more grievous by the very fact that, as a remedy, God allows men to fall into other sins.[42]

Sometimes the most heart-wrenching prayers are those said in longing for God's mercy and his deliverance from a debilitating addiction. Such confessions are deep communion with God. And if we are predisposed to pride, they may be the only communion we would otherwise seek with him. God is quite willing to let you and me deal with alcoholism, a poor self-image, masturbation, and anger — if only these failures move us to reach out for life again. If our ugly behaviors drive us to our knees, they are more beautiful than the outwardly clean yet empty facade that drives us into the desert to die alone.

"Blessed are the poor in spirit, for theirs is the kingdom of heaven."

Though we all lack the most basic kind of life within, Jesus began the Sermon on the Mount with good news. He said that despite our failures and inadequacies, God is not far from anyone, at any time. God's love penetrates even the darkest holes you and I dig for ourselves. All may seem murky. The hope in our hearts may have left years ago. We may be holding up signs that no one wants to read. We may be holding spoons with no one to feed us or to be fed by us. It is often from these depths below, where everything looks dark and chaotic — and not in the lights above — that we hear the voice that spoke our world into existence *still* saying, "It is not good for you to be alone. I will be your helper."

May we breathe deeply.

2

ENVY AND
THE MOURNER

"Real isn't how you are made," said the Skin Horse. "It's a thing that happens to you....

"It doesn't happen all at once .... You become. It takes a long time. That's why it doesn't often happen to people who break easily, or have sharp edges, or who have to be carefully kept. Generally, by the time you are Real, most of your hair has been loved off, and your eyes drop out and you get loose in the joints and very shabby. But these things don't matter at all, because once you are Real you can't be ugly, except to people who don't understand."

THE SKIN HORSE, IN *The Velveteen Rabbit*

I GOT TO SLEEP UNTIL 7:20 THIS MORNING, AND IT WAS GLORIOUS. The last time that happened was exactly two and a half years ago. Those were the days before our first son was born.

Augie is an early riser. Three in the morning was his favorite time to start the day for a while. He got all the way to 5:00 a.m. by the time he was one, and then his new brother started getting up at 3:00. Now they both sleep until about 6:00. I used to be a morning person who would tap my time before work for the pleasures of pressed coffee and reading on my back porch, but no more. Now I have two alarm clocks, and they can't be set to a new time. I have offered the boys cars, monster Lego sets, and permission to beat my computer with their fists (which they seem to enjoy very much) if only they would sleep in. But no. Our boys wake up two or three hours before I would like to, and then we start the hard mornings.

My wife leaves our home early for work, so it's just me juggling a two-year-old and one-year-old. Neither of our boys wakes up gracefully. They begin wailing the moment they think it's time to rise, each seeming to say, "Dad! I'm really, really tired still! Come get me out of bed! Otherwise I might fall back to sleep again like a normal person!" There's nothing like being woken up before the sun rises, only to be yelled at for an hour straight as you change soiled diapers, dress grouchy bodies, and remind your assailants that breakfast often takes more than thirty seconds to make. Sometimes I think I just wasn't built to be a stay-at-home mom.

I'm always exhausted by the time Kel returns at noon to take over so I can begin one of my three jobs. She feels the same way when I return. Over the last few years, our kids and our routine have taken a real toll. Kelly and I joke that we don't know what we fought about before we had children, but we fight now. Vibrantly. Because of the constant emotional drain we experience, because we each tug for alone time, and because we are both just plain selfish sometimes, it now seems as though we trade harsh words nearly every day.

Often I hear the things my colleagues are concerned with, and I begin to hurt inside. "If I could have their life for a week," I think to myself, "with all their so-called pains and difficulties, I would be in bliss." I can almost picture my nervous system healing, my work getting done occasionally, or my taking a day off without feeling guilty that somewhere my wife is utterly exhausted. Recently, I told a friend that I hate my life right now — that it's grinding me down and I feel like I can't escape. I have nothing to cut. All I can do is hurt, and hurting leads me to constant resentment. This is not how things should be. The life I have is just subpar. God certainly screwed up when he took me down this road.

And of course it's all a lie. Things I think are trials now will one day be joys to reminisce about. The difficulties I experience now are achieving good for my soul. My selfishness is losing its hold. I am becoming increasingly aware of others. I have a healthy, happy family and many healthy, happy relationships. My life is truly blessed.

But *envy* doesn't care. It wants to kill me, and this is as good a place to start as any.

Envy suggests I look at those around me and consider their free time, their paycheck, their successes, their love life — and envy says to me, "The life you have is worthless. Do whatever it takes to escape it." This is the essence of envy. It rejects the good life God has given me and obsesses over what God gives someone else.

This may seem petty or trivial, but it is lethal. Envy has the deadly ability to distract my heart and mind from the daily bread God puts in my hands each morning, focusing me instead on the gifts, status, talents, and joys he gives to others. This is not only a rejection of the good that God has given to me; this is a desire to become someone I'm not, was never made to be, and will not enjoy becoming if my jealousy ever were to succeed.

More pernicious still, envy points to the good things that other people have while hiding the difficulties these people face. Envy insists that everyone but me is happy — that no one else hurts or struggles or wants like I do. And when envy has shown you and me these images, it yells into our minds that our lives are not valuable. In short, envy treats this God-given life as so much trash — all because it doesn't contain more money, more toys, more vacations, more acclaim, more sleep, more success, more health, more privileges.

In the Scriptures' most dramatic depiction of envy, a whole nation decided they no longer wanted to follow God.[1] Israel envied the nations around them that had a human ruler. The Israelites had been told that God was their king, but now they wanted a king they could see. God understood the complaint and mourned in response: "They have rejected me as their king."[2] It may be one of the most important passages in the Old Testament, for the remainder of the Hebrew Scriptures shows a tragic downward spiral. The nation did not want to be its own unique self, a people led by God and called to bless all the world. The people wanted a human ruler who would tax them heavily, drive their sons in front of his chariots, and serve his own lusts over the good of the people.

Desiring to be somebody else, Israel ripped in two almost at once,[3] and over time each half was conquered by foreign forces, with the people taken from their homeland in chains. The envy of the Israelites led them to reject their identity, and when they no longer knew who they were, the nation split and was conquered, and the people were led off into foreign lands.

Whenever the Bible speaks of this kind of movement to foreign lands — either forced or chosen — it is called *exile.* In the ancient world, exile was the ultimate punishment. Removal from one's family, one's culture, and one's homeland was a fate worse than death, for it meant a hard, lonely life separated from all one knew and loved. Exile took everything a person had. Exile was separation from all that was good. And each time the Bible describes an exile, it *always* begins with envy.

Consider the story of Adam and Eve. Eve wanted a status that God had reserved for himself: knowledge of good and evil. Eve and her husband violated God's good world to get it, so God removed them from the garden of Eden. Their envy led to exile.[4]

In the story of Adam and Eve's children, Cain wanted to be esteemed like his brother, Abel. Cain envied the status Abel received, but instead of doing the things that would gain it for himself, Cain killed his brother. When God saw what Cain did, he removed Cain from the land he loved and told Cain he would be a restless wanderer the rest of his life. Envy led to murder, and murder led to exile.[5]

Consider the story of Jacob. Jacob envied the blessing his father intended to give to his older brother, Esau, so Jacob deceived his father and stole Esau's birthright. Because of his theft, Jacob had to leave his home and family, fleeing to a foreign land. His envy led to betrayal, and his betrayal led to exile.[6]

And we're told that the Devil envied God's power and God's glory. Failing to overthrow God, the Devil was cast out of heaven. Envy led to rebellion, and rebellion led to exile.[7]

I could go on and on, but the pattern is always the same. In each case, exile is the natural state of envy, because envy separates us from who we were made to be and the life we were made to enjoy. Envy is the sin that insists we transform into something we are not; and when I am separated from myself, I become truly lost.

You and I know what envy looks like. For some of us, it creeps up when we ride in someone else's car, eat at someone else's house, hear where they went on vacation, or hear that they didn't go on vacation and now they're out of debt. For some of us, it is looking at someone else's family and their remarkable lack of issues. For some it is seeing some no-talent guy hold the job we want. For some of us, envy begins speaking in the checkout lane when we see airbrushed bodies of celebrities or the gadgets they hold with manicured fingers. Among the many things envy loves to point out to me are the successes and attention that my friends experience in their writing and ministry. While they enjoy marks of success and growth that are praiseworthy and beautiful, I look from a distance and wonder, *Why not me?*

And those are envy's three favorite words.

The answer is that the lives I look at from afar are not mine. They belong to others. They're filled with different struggles, different obstacles, and different experiences of God. Those around me are growing in different ways, with different stories. Their souls need to be repaired in different places, and their talents are made to serve different people. They are not on my path, and I am not on theirs. I need to grow in other places. I need different kinds of surgery.

Envy rejects such answers. It insists I direct myself away from the only life worth having — the one that God is presently giving me. Envy invites you and me to put on glasses that see the world as though God has not given us everything we need to be fully drenched in his redeeming, soul-restoring, son- and daughter-creating, joy-producing, exquisitely wonderful love. Envy is a deadly sin because it inspires us to say to God, "The life you've given me *just isn't good enough.* I need a new set of widgets. I need to be worry-free. I need to have a different life with different perks."

Socrates called envy "the ulcer of the soul."[8] It is the only deadly sin that offers nothing but pain; and like the masochists we are, we take it and ask for more. Envy leads to exile because envy is the desire for life on my own terms, my own energy, my own course — on my own, without the reign of God.

We prefer a king we can see, and the one staring back at us from our bathroom mirror seems like a fine candidate.

The Eccentric Landowner

Jesus told his disciples a story of a landowner who went out early in the morning to hire men to work in his fields.[9] He agreed to pay them a day's wage for a day's worth of work, and they happily agreed. The landowner's fields were large and still in need of more workers, so a few hours later when he saw more men standing around, he said, "You also go and work in my vineyard, and I will pay you whatever is right."[10] Three hours later he hired more men — and three hours after that, still more. When evening came, he began paying all the workers in his vineyard, but he gave them each a full day's wage.

When those who had been hired in the early morning realized they had been paid the same as those hired just an hour before the day ended, they began to grumble.[11] "These men who were hired last worked only one hour," they complained. "And you have made them equal to us who have borne the burden of the work and the heat of the day."[12]

But the landowner frowned and said to one of them, "Friend, I am not being unfair to you. Didn't you agree to work for a denarius [a day's wage]? Take your pay and go. I want to give the one who was hired last the same as I gave you. Don't I have the right to do what I want with my own money? Or are you envious because I am generous?"[13]

Though today we use the term *friend* to display fondness, the landowner used it here as a rebuke.[14] The worker was not invited to hang around. He was not offered dinner. He was told to take his pay and go. He was separated from the landowner and the other workers. We could even say he was cast out of the landowner's garden. At the end of the story, the landowner notes the reason: the worker was envious of another man's blessing. Of course, the landowner represents God, and leaving God's garden is the movement of Adam and Eve. It is the withdrawal into exile.

In the vineyard story, Jesus taught that God's grace on the undeserving is a reason for joy and a cause for celebration.[15] In fact, Jesus thought this grace was so important that in his story, the words of the grumbling worker were an insult to everyone else in the garden, requiring the worker's dismissal. Jesus suggested that those who do not share the landowner's enthusiasm have missed the whole point of being in the garden. Yes, God is calling everyone to work in his fields. Yes, there is a reward that accompanies such work, but the reward is not a paycheck bigger than someone else's. *The reward is participat-*

ing in the only life there actually is. The reward is the invitation back into the garden. The invitation to work is grace, and you and I cannot receive anything above and beyond that.

Thus, when this worker envied those who did not work as hard or as long as he did, he was choosing to no longer participate in the life of heaven. He preferred a different kind of life, one separate from these undeserving workers who entered the garden at such a late hour. And as with the other parables, when someone does not enjoy the life of heaven, they are offered the door.

Not long after Jesus told the story of the workers in the vineyard, the mother of two of Jesus' disciples came to speak with him. Her request went something like this: "When you are enthroned, allow my two sons here to take the seats at your right and left hand."[16] And her boys affirmed that, yes, those were the positions they wanted.

Whenever I have sought a position of authority such as Head of State, I have always found that it's best to get my mom to ask for the spot. (It works smashingly.) But in this case, Jesus said to the family, "You don't know what you are asking."[17] And this is the response God gives all of us when we push for what he has not given us.

We must be careful what we wish for. Ambition is certainly not bad. A life without ambitions suffers from sloth, but the two disciples in this story failed to *understand* their desires, for when Jesus was enthroned for the world to see, it was not on some golden pedestal in some fancy palace. He was nailed to a Roman cross, and the men at his left and right were likewise hanging from planks of wood.

If there was something that was actually good for me, certainly the God who loves me would provide it. Psalm 23 — perhaps the most famous song ever composed — begins, "The LORD is my shepherd, I lack nothing."[18] Too often, however, you and I think that our supreme good is a healthy body, a bigger paycheck, a life without struggle. But in God's eyes, your good and mine is first and foremost about our character, about our soul-health, about making us like Jesus — and God never misses an opportunity to bring us such good. Sometimes the sicknesses we experience may actually benefit our souls. Sometimes the poverty we undergo gives us what is most valuable — wisdom, contentment, and freedom. In fact, Jesus said it is those who appear to have everything who are the true objects of pity.[19]

The irony continues to build in this story of the two disciples and their mom. When the other ten disciples heard about the request, they were indignant. Why? They had not thought to ask for the positions themselves, and now these two brothers stood to gain what they deserved to have. Jesus cut their discussion short, saying, "You know that the rulers of the Gentiles lord it over them, and their high officials exercise authority over them. Not so with you. Instead, whoever wants to become great among you must be your servant, and whoever wants to be first must be your slave — just as the Son of Man did not come to be served, but to serve, and to give his life as a ransom for many."[20]

This is Jesus' word on envy. He showed his disciples that envy always targets positions and possessions that exile us from others, but those who would be like Jesus will turn from such pursuits and serve others. They will build relationships instead of seeking opportunities to dominate. They will engage others instead of ostracizing themselves because of their grandiose ambitions. The blessed life is the one that seeks the good of others first, for the blessed life *is* one that is united with others. There is no other blessed kind of life.

You and I experience a curse when we envy, for envy drives us into exile — away from others, away from community, and thus away from the kingdom of heaven. In the end, envy proves to be the sin of the insecure and the beggarly. The envious workers who came to the landowner assumed he considered them less worthy than those who received the same pay for less work. The disciples who grumbled at the two brothers assumed the brothers' gain would mean their loss. Envy resents being just a little lower than someone else, because the envious are not comfortable in their own skin. Envy is how sin mourns, and it provides no satisfaction or pleasure.

Those who mourn in this way will never be comforted.

SHARED SCARS

On Thursday nights I get together with five or six other teachers for food and drinks at Greeley's best Mexican restaurant. We listen to each other's stories. We talk about life. But most of our time is spent discussing how Jesus' teachings affect our course of study. We have a couple of grad students and a few recent graduates; I teach philosophy; and then there's Trish, who teaches anthropology. Trish is a vibrant person whose enthusiasm often guides our conversations, but that changed recently when Trish's daughter Ashley was in a near-fatal car wreck.

Ashley's ribs and pelvis were shattered in the accident, but worst of all, she hit her head awkwardly and sustained a serious brain injury. Trish came back to our group for the first time last week and said that right now Ashley is functioning at just 70 percent of her past mental acuity. At one point when explaining Ashley's injuries, Trish slowed her pace to avoid crying and said that even though it was a technical term, some doctors had begun referring to her daughter's brain as "retarded."

I generally push our conversations along, but with that word in the air, everything was quiet. We each felt a deep sense of loss for our friend. Trish was on the verge of breakdown when I heard a voice to my right.

"I have a retarded brain."

Not only is Tom a graduate student in mathematics; he possesses a brilliant wit and a wonderful personality. It is difficult to see the connection between God and high-level calculus, but Tom can draw the lines. When speaking with Tom, you are immediately aware that you're interacting with a coherent, likable person who is so often filled with joy that it's, well, enviable.

"Yeah, when I was a kid, I got hit in the head with a golf club," Tom said, pointing to the scar hidden by his long hair. As Tom shared his story, whatever force the word *retarded* carried just moments before suddenly evaporated. One man sharing his scar crushed the term underfoot.

Author Rob Bell suggests that the two most powerful words in our language are "me too," because when someone else shares our pain, we are no longer alone.[21] *We need to know that others hurt with us, for tragedies — like sin — have the power to send us into exile.* They not only bring us grief; tragedies separate us from those who don't understand.

Yet when we listen to the stories of those who have been where we are — when we listen to pain overcome and victory won over time — we move from exile back into community. The scars of others are signs that we are not alone and that healing is possible, *for scars are wounds filled in with living flesh.* Scars are voids overcome with life, and they bear witness that God can raise to life again those who have been pierced.

A few years ago, my mom thought she had breast cancer. It hit me hard, and I brought the concern to my church. The pastor asked if anyone would pray for my mom, and on the other side of the room, a large arm went up. It was Jay's. Jay is an enormous man who nearly died when cancer ate its way up from his neck into his face. His body had been free of cancer for a few years, and on that day he stood up and walked my way. Jay can bench somewhere in the neighborhood of five hundred pounds, and that morning as he sat with me, sharing his story and praying for my mom, it felt as though he lifted all the weight I was carrying. The scars on his neck were signs that God can raise to life again those who have been pierced.

The Bible tells the story of a man named Thomas, who lost his teacher. Evil men killed him, and Thomas left everyone he knew to hide and weep. It seemed that his future, his joy, and all his hope had been taken from him. Instead of joining others who felt the same loss, Thomas chose to hurt on his own, suffer on his own, deal with it on his own. He let his pain lead him into exile.

But then his friends found him. They pursued him in his pain and brought him hope. "We have seen the Lord!" they said.[22] But Thomas would not believe. "There is no hope in times like this," he must have thought. It would take far more than another man's word to lift him out of exile.

He would need to see scars.

Soon after, Thomas was meeting with his friends again when Jesus walked into the room. Jesus said, "Peace be with you!"[23] and invited Thomas to come and feel the wounds in his wrists and to touch the open gash in his side, and suddenly Thomas's pain was transformed. The scars bore witness that God raises to life again those who have been pierced.

Comfort cannot come in exile. It cannot come when we isolate ourselves from others and bury our pain. Comfort cannot come when we let go of our restraints and eat whatever we want, sleep with whomever we want, drink whatever we want, or worse. Comfort comes only when we draw close to other human beings who will walk through tragedy with us and remind us that God raises to life again those who have been pierced.

Whether our pain is due to tragedy or our own failure, we must share our hurts with others. Hiding is suicidal.

This is especially true when we mourn our failures. Sometimes we feel unworthy or dirty because of the things we have done. Sometimes we do not enter healthy relationships because we think, "If that person knew the problems I have or the things I have done or the thoughts I have when I'm alone, they wouldn't spend five minutes with me." Sometimes it is our sin that separates us — not because we have wronged someone else, but because we are ashamed. Sometimes the biggest barrier between us and others is simply our self-image. We mourn who we are and dwell in that state of mourning until it becomes our permanent home.

This is why Jesus' brother James wrote, "Confess your sins to each other ... so that you may be healed."[24]

In both grief from loss and bereavement from failure, the return from exile is always about confession — sharing where we hurt, sharing where we fail. When God confronted Adam and Eve with their deed, he gave them an opportunity to simply tell their story and come clean.[25] Because they would not, they were released into exile. When God came to Cain and asked what he had done, Cain pretended he knew nothing of his brother's murder, and God released him into exile. Yet when Jacob chose to quit running from Esau and confessed his failure to his brother, he was received back into the land of his ancestors.[26]

And when it was time to ask God to return to Israel to lead his people again as their King, John the Baptist invited the nation out to the Jordan River. He dunked them in the waters as a symbol of their desire for God's return as King, and those who repented with John were the first to hear Jesus. They were the first to see God heal the broken. They were the first to see God lift up the paralyzed. They were the first to be told that Israel's long exile was over, "for the kingdom of heaven has come near."[27]

While the exiled are abandoned, the comforted are drawn close. While the exiled are unknown, the comforted know love. While the exiled are alone, the comforted are at peace.

THE BLESSED MOURNER

Three years ago, I had a job working for a home builder. All day long I sat at a desk waiting to show houses, but this wasn't your normal real estate office. This was a trailer on wheels — with no plumbing — situated in the middle of a field somewhere in northern Colorado. In a typical week, I saw maybe one human being, and he generally wore a uniform and carried mail. After a couple of years, it became a depressing, lonely job.

One morning I got an email from the head of the philosophy department at the local university, saying he had an immediate opening for a teaching position. I had to start in four days — but could I do it? This was a pivotal moment for me. I'd been steadily working to get such a job for half a decade. My wife and I had sacrificed much for my extra schooling and our move to Greeley. Not only that — our family had just lost a substantial part of our income and had no way to make it up. We'd been praying for a break, and this was it! This was divine work on our behalf! I immediately wrote back, saying, "Yes, I'll take it!" I started getting everything prepared and in place — babysitters lined up, schedules adjusted, and so on.

But a few hours later, the department head responded with bad news. He said that he was in such a panic to fill the spot that he had invited someone else to teach the courses before he got my reply. The job had been filled, but not by me.

It was January, and my New Year's resolution to stop swearing was quickly torched. I went outside and kicked a big fat dent in the Homes Available sign in front of my office. (For the next few weeks there was a big boot mark in the middle, causing the sign to read "Ho*es Available.") For a few hours I had no appetite. I didn't want to talk to or see anyone. I didn't want to be anywhere or do anything. I had no clue how to handle something so important falling through my hands like this.[28]

Of course, my story is fairly tame. What do we say to those whose mourning goes far deeper — to those who have lost a baby or a spouse? Or to those who have lost their home? Or to those whose children have suffered major injuries such as brain trauma?

Often there is nothing we can say — and often that is best.

Later that week, I arrived late for a weekly breakfast with a bunch of guys. I took my seat, and the leader, Rick, asked, "So how's it going?" This wasn't a mere hello. Rick is the kind of guy who actually wants to know. There I sat, burdened and depressed, and I looked at everyone around the table and said, "Nothing worth talking about." I was aching inside. I was in exile, and I chose to offer that pathetic answer to someone who genuinely wanted to listen. I opted for the darkness outside.

And that's not how things should work.

As Jesus gave the Beatitudes, he looked out at his audience, a ragtag bunch who certainly had undergone their fair share of trials. And as he considered the work of his Father all throughout our world, he said categorically, "Blessed are those who mourn, for they will be comforted."[29]

It took me another few days to share with my community of friends the story of the lost job. During our talk, Rick said that he, too, had major job concerns. In fact, nearly everyone at our breakfast was in need of — and lacking — financial security. You could tell from then on that we shared a new trust. A new reliance. A new understanding. And in our mourning we found comfort.

Envy and mourning are both responses to the places we lack. Both those who envy and those who mourn are in positions of want. They both desire a different kind of life with different details, but only one group finds happiness. More than anything else, those who mourn expose their pain. They confess it. They allow others with ointments and bandages to see it. They open themselves up to receive help, and in those spaces there is healing. Mourning is not a place devoid of life. As Oscar Wilde wrote, "Where there is sorrow there is holy ground."[30]

3

SLOTH AND THOSE WHO HUNGER FOR A LIFE MADE RIGHT

Let others complain that the age is wicked;
my complaint is that it is wretched, for it lacks passion.
SØREN KIERKEGAARD

When I teach Introduction to Philosophy, I begin with a story about Al. Al is a man of average ability, average means, and average intelligence. One day Al reads in the newspaper that the local university is looking for volunteers for an experiment that will "surely transform your life." When Al decides to see what it's all about, the scientists conducting the experiment tell him, "We are going to remove your brain and nervous system, and we'll insert them into this machine. You will then experience a life of unlimited success and pleasure. To you, it will feel like real life, but we will be directing it all from out here." Given his average life, Al doesn't think he has much to lose, and so he signs the forms and plugs in.

Once in the machine, Al realizes he has amazing new abilities. He tries out for a local football team and blows everyone away. He becomes a professional quarterback, winning one championship after another. He uses his fame to lead multiple businesses to wealth and renown. When he retires, he decides to run for public office, and in no time Al becomes president. After two successful terms, he retreats to the Bahamas to live out his remaining days — rich, respected, and well loved. Of course it's all an illusion. Chemicals are simply causing Al's brain to make him think he is living this fantastic life.

After sharing this made-up story, I ask my class, "So would you like to be Al?"

It's a difficult question. Who wouldn't want to experience a life of outlandish wealth, fame, and success — even if it was make-believe? But there is something else in us that says even if I could experience every pleasure imaginable, I want my life to be real. By entering the scientists' machine, I would neglect everything that actually matters. By signing up, I would be choosing total indifference toward my friends, my family, and my role in the *real* world.

This is a fitting analogy for *sloth*. At its core, sloth moves us away from everything that ultimately matters and directs us toward simple distractions. Sloth is not mere laziness. Sloth is indifference — indifference toward my soul, my neighbors, my world, or my God. Drug users, TiVo addicts, and obsessive video gamers may be poisoned by sloth, but so are most workaholics.[1] Sloth is not restfulness. Sloth is escapism of the deadly sort. Sloth saps our time and emotions through a favorite sports team, a new set of shoes, or obsession over our appearance — while leaving scant energy for our marriage or kids or duties. In fact, sloth is best expressed not by a lazy attitude but in zeal over petty matters. Pascal wrote, "The same man who spends so many days and nights in fury and despair at losing some office or at some imaginary affront to his honor is the very one who knows that he is going to lose everything through death but feels neither anxiety nor emotion. It is a monstrous thing to see one and the same heart at once so sensitive to minor things and so strangely insensitive to the greatest."[2]

Nothing is so clearly modern, so clearly Western, as is sloth.[3] Despite our fast-moving, success-worshiping, ulcer-ridden society, we invest our energies and talents most often in what is trivial. Despite our frantic pace, our eyes are seldom focused on what is actually good.

Sloth, in fact, is a sorrow about goodness. It finds those things that we were made to enjoy and pursue to be useless and boring instead. Sloth tells us that the good life is dull, and when we believe such lies, we are in a bad spot indeed. As Jesus said, "If your eyes are unhealthy, your whole body will be full of darkness. If then the light within you is darkness, how great is that darkness!"[4]

Dante correctly called sloth a failure to love God with all our heart, mind, and soul,[5] and thus sloth is antithetical to what Jesus painted as the heaven-born life. We should think of sloth as a hell-like condition, for those given to it fail to live. Sloth is content to aim us toward either apathy or fanaticism. *All that matters is that the target is worthless.*

Sloth slides into our lifestyles more easily (and unannounced) than any of the other deadly sins. Both the religious and the secular use the talents graciously given by God for boring, ultimately meaningless pursuits without a second thought. We should not picture sloth as a laid-back coach potato. (Soul-restoring, celebratory rest is a major part of the well-lived life.) Sloth is more like the grim reaper. It is the messenger of death, who, with bony fingers, pokes the spots in our lives that ought to be thriving and causes them to atrophy.

BURIAL

During the last week of his life, Jesus told a difficult story in which a slave master going on a long trip entrusted his property to his three slaves.[6] To each he gave a handful of coins called "talents." In Jesus' day, a single talent was the amount a good worker might earn over the course of twenty years. A talent was the price of a nice home. It was the price of a good slave. A talent in the hands of these men represented the value of their freedom and the span of half their working years. Thus, when the master in this story entrusted his talents to these slaves, he left them with their very lives in hand.

All three slaves chose not to flee with the money. They wanted to stay in their master's home, and while the master was gone, the first two servants doubled the amount they had been given. When their master returned, he said something absolutely unique: "Well done, good and faithful servant! You have been faithful with a few things; I will put you in charge of many things. Come and share your master's happiness!"[7]

This praise was an unheard-of elevation in status. Slaves were always inferior to masters, yet in Jesus' story the faithful slaves were lifted into the same kind of life, the same kind of joy, as that experienced by their master. They were invited into his company and pleasure as though they were sons.

The third slave, however, did not invest his master's money. He did not use the talent he had been given. When asked what he did with the money, the slave said, "I was afraid and went out and hid your gold in the ground."[8] The master looked at the slave whom he had called into service and whom he desired to share in his bliss and said, "Throw that worthless servant outside, into the darkness."[9]

By burying the talent, the slave showed what he thought of the master and his master's pursuits. They were dead to him. Their proper place was six feet under. The master did not hesitate to rid himself of a slave like that. Surely the slave was once valuable, but his heart had grown far from the master's concerns, so he was cast away. This was Jesus' response to sloth. And as with the other deadly sins, Jesus paired it with hell.

The failure of the third slave in Jesus' story is his inactivity. He is a "lazy servant."[10] Thus, anticipating God's return is not about retreating to safe confines where we bunker down as the world destroys itself. Waiting is not about receding from the world for the remainder of our lives to focus on inner holiness. Rather, *waiting is about taking what has been given to us — grace, mercy, love, joy, hope — and multiplying it.* This is active preparation.[11] This is how the hopeful get ready for God's return.

Conversely, those who bury the lives God has given them are cast away. The slave who neglected the talent entrusted to him was no better than one who simply fled when his master was gone. Both would end up in the same place — the darkness outside, away from the life of the master. This is no small teaching, for it suggests that what you and I *do* now is of supreme value in God's eyes.

Jesus told two other stories similar to this one and with similar conclusions. The first was about a king preparing a wedding banquet for his son.[12] When no one showed up, he invited the poor and desperate, the good and bad from the street corners to come and fill his wedding celebration. But when people began to come, he noticed one without wedding clothes. This man was too lazy to dress for the wonderful occasion, so the king told his servants to "tie him hand and foot, and throw him outside, into the darkness."[13] As before with the slave master, in order to stay inside with the king, one had to be passionate about the king's concerns.

And in Jesus' final parable in Matthew's gospel — the story following the one about the talents — Jesus spoke of a time to come in which everyone will stand before him and be separated like sheep and goats.[14] To some Jesus will say, "Come, you who are blessed by my Father; take your inheritance." To others he will say, "Depart from me, you who are cursed."[15] In this story, as with the other two, God receives the blessed like siblings who experience his kind of happiness; but the cursed are thrown out, cast away from his life. When both the blessed and the cursed ask why they are entering their given future, "the King will reply, 'Truly I tell you, whatever you did [or did not do] for one of the least of these brothers and sisters of mine, you did [or did not do] for me.'"[16]

What did the blessed do? They fed the hungry, clothed the naked, cared for the infirm, visited the imprisoned. They saw human beings, made in the image of God, and responded. In Jesus' final story, those who cared for the needy cared about that which matters most to God. Rejecting a life of free rein outside, they joined God like the two servants who faithfully multiplied their talents.

The common thread running through all three stories is the rejection of sloth. The blessed are passionate about what really matters — the image of God in those around them. They could remain seated, but instead they rise and invest themselves in that which ultimately matters.

Conversely, those who fail to act get shown the door. Jesus' stories demonstrate that the alternative to living with an awareness of what is good — to valuing what God deems valuable — is the darkness outside. Those who do not engage what is good — who participate only in the voids of our world and not the beautiful world that God is reconstructing — are by nature outside. They fail to participate in the only reality there is.

Heaven and hell are displayed most vibrantly in our passions and our indifference. Heaven is the sphere in which generosity is normal, and the indifferent prove to all that they have no place there. Far from kindness being a moral duty that we grudgingly perform in order to get into the afterlife, kindness and generosity, grace and care, *are* the life of heaven. Those who will not rise to enjoy them will not enjoy heaven.

DISORIENTED DESIRES

There's an ancient story about humanity trying to leave our world in order to invade God's dwelling place. They began building a grand tower that would stretch into the sky. "Come," they said, "let us build ourselves a city, with a tower that reaches to the heavens, so that we may make a name for ourselves and not be scattered over the face of the whole earth."[17] It seems like a worthwhile desire. Who really wants to stay and fill this world anyway?[18] Isn't the point of my faith to escape the world — to go to heaven and be with God?

What is fascinating about this story is that God does not want his children to journey upward to be with him. In fact, God reacts against their tower and their desires in a dramatic way. He miraculously confuses the language of these people so they can no longer communicate, and then he scatters them across the globe. Apparently this desire to escape our world was so bad that it moved God to take extreme measures to put it down.

But why? Why is it a bad thing to want to go and be with God? Why *not* build a tower that reaches to the heavens? On one front, God acted mercifully. Human beings can't survive in outer space, and that is where a really, really tall tower would lead. But more important still, the story shows that removing humanity from this earth so they can "go to heaven" is not on God's agenda. The predominant theme of the Bible is actually the opposite. We are not to work our way to God, because God longs to enter our sphere and make his home with us. The duty of humanity is not to climb a ladder to get to heaven, but to prepare our world, our lives, our hearts, so that when God enters them, he will be most welcome.

The God of the Bible consistently draws near to those he loves to make his home with them. Notice, God drew near to Adam and Eve as one walking in the cool of the day.[19] He drew near to the Hebrew people leaving Egypt in the pillar of fire.[20] He drew near to the Jewish refugees in the desert as a glorious cloud filling their tabernacle.[21] He drew near to the nation of Israel in the *shekinah* glory of the temple.[22] He drew near to Shadrach, Meshach, and Abednego in the fires of Babylon.[23] And the great climax of all human history was God becoming flesh and dwelling among us in Christ.[24]

Over and again, God moves toward us — into our sphere, into our problems and circumstances. It seems, in fact, that God's chief desire is to dwell with those who long for him.[25]

Notice, those building the Tower of Babel pursued the opposite course. Their desire was to make their name great, to announce to the world their triumph as they stormed the gates of heaven. It looks rather pharisaical in fact, that somehow one's ability to gain heaven should resound all over the world. Of such projects, the prophet Habakkuk asked, "Has not the LORD Almighty determined that the people's labor is only fuel for the fire, that the nations exhaust themselves for nothing? *For the earth will be filled with the knowledge of the glory of the LORD as the waters cover the sea.*"[26]

Conversely, Jesus told stories of the faithful preparing for the return of a lover, a king, a savior.[27] The movement of the faithful is to make their space ready, not to abandon it. We misunderstand what heaven is when we think of it as a place to which we will escape. Heaven is instead the sphere of God, and his great desire is to unite that sphere with our world. In fact, the parallel story to the Tower of Babel occurs in the New Testament at the beginning of Acts:

When the day of Pentecost came, [Christ-followers] were all to-gether in one place. Suddenly a sound like the blowing of a vio-lent wind came from heaven and *filled* the whole house where they were sitting. They saw what seemed to be tongues of fire that separated and came to rest on each of them. All of them were *filled* with the Holy Spirit and began to speak in other tongues as the Spirit enabled them.

Now there were staying in Jerusalem God-fearing Jews from every nation under heaven. When they heard this sound, a crowd came together in bewilderment, because each one heard their own language being spoken. Utterly amazed, they asked: "Aren't all these who are speaking Galileans? Then how is it that each of us hears them in our native language?... We hear them declar-ing the wonders of God in our own tongues!"[28]

The movement of God is to fill. While at Babel the people wanted to escape the world, at Pentecost God entered it. At Babel the lan-guages were confused, yet at Pentecost the multilinguistic people began hearing a new unifying message. At Babel a select group sought to make their name great across the earth, and at Pentecost this desire was again reversed as God's name was made great by those prepared to go into "Judea and Samaria, and to the ends of the earth" with good news for all people.[29]

We should read that when God's Spirit was unleashed into our world at Pentecost and rested on the faithful like tongues of fire, the curse of Babel was broken. No longer would cultural barriers, creeds, or histories separate confused humanity, for there was a new language that all people could speak freely to one another — the lan-guage of God's inbreaking reign. What these early Christians spoke was the gospel — the news that because of Jesus, death was dying, sin was failing, and heaven was slowly beginning to fill the earth as it was filling them.

So too, Christian theology does not climax with this world being destroyed. It climaxes with this world being filled.[30] Pentecost is a sign of God's future. As we saw in the parable of the sower, God is now filling a world that looks barren, like a sower planting a magic seed in his garden. And miraculously we see that even the rough and abused ground is suddenly beginning to overflow with new life. The poor in spirit are finding the kingdom of heaven; the meek are inheriting God's world; the mourning are finding comfort. It seems that all the old and broken rules no longer apply.

As Jesus transitions from the first four beatitudes (each focused on those lacking) to the last four beatitudes (each focused on the marginalized faithful), he inserts this idea of being filled. This is the climax to the Beatitudes. This is the high point. God is working to see our world abound with the kind of life that he has. God is presently entering the hearts and minds, the communities and relationships, of broken human beings. This is the solution to the sin problem. This is the gospel.

Jesus notes that this flood of God's presence and rule will begin with longing. The arrival of God's reign will begin with desire, for he said, "Blessed are those who hunger and thirst for righteousness, for they will be filled."[31]

In my life and in yours, God's presence enters only when we are empty enough to receive it.

STARVED

Not long ago I went with seven other guys on a seven-mile backpacking trip in Rocky Mountain National Park. For some, it was their first time camping without a car nearby. One of the last to sign up for the trip was Eric. Eric is from Texas, and he had never been camping before. We set out on the trail, and it soon became obvious that Eric was a bit slower than everyone else. When we stopped to eat, I looked through his bag and saw twelve large cans of food he had brought for his meals. Generally, when you are carrying all your clothes, food, and gear up a mountainside, you want your pack to be as light as possible. So twenty pounds worth of canned soup and pineapples aren't the best choice.

By mile six of our hike, Eric had drifted to the back and was slowing down the whole group. It was beginning to get dark, so we decided that half the group would go set up the campsite, and the slower walkers would get there when they could. I stayed behind to direct the stragglers, but as things got dark, I missed an important turn and took the few aching, exhausted novices an extra two miles past our destination. One thousand extra vertical feet up the side of a mountain.

Once the sun had set, it became clear that I missed the turn somewhere, and we headed back down. Exhausted and hungry, we moved through the dark with one headlamp to share among the four of us. We were so discouraged that all we could find to talk about was food — the types of meals we had brought and how it was going to be so good to sit and fill our bellies again. For Eric, it took a superhuman effort to carry all those cans that far.

When we finally arrived at the campsite, everyone cheered. There was a fire. Meals were being cooked, and Eric rifled through his bag to find a single can of Campbell's Chunky Sirloin Burger, the treasure he had hauled for eleven miles. He lifted the can and relished the picture of steaming soup on its front, and then he paused. His brow turned down, and he looked at the group sitting around the fire eating their rehydrated meals out of lightweight, rippable bags. He exhaled a long, melancholy breath and asked simply, "Does anyone have a can opener?"

Had someone not brought a Swiss army knife, I imagine there would have been an interesting display of passion, as Eric almost certainly would have thrown the can across the campsite and proceeded to beat the innards out with a sharp rock. It would have been embarrassing. Those watching would have told the story for years to come. But there are times when our hunger is so great we will do nearly anything to appease it.

I remember renting the movie *Alive* on a day I had set aside to fast for a friend of mine. The movie tells the true story of a South American soccer team whose plane went down in the Andes. Only half the people survived the crash, and after they buried the bodies of their fellow passengers in snowfields surrounding the wreckage, the survivors began to starve. After waiting many days, it became apparent to the survivors that no one was coming to their rescue. As they counted their options, the survivors started debating the ethics of cooking and eating the buried human bodies in the snow. They talked for days, asking if it was natural, whether it was right or wrong. I remember watching the movie, my own stomach empty, and thinking, "Eat the people! Just eat the people!" I guess I don't fast well. A single day of starvation, and eating corpses had become perfectly acceptable. But there are times when our hunger is so great that we will do nearly anything to appease it.

In the story of the prodigal son,[32] the younger son returns not because he realizes how much he loves his father but because he is hungry. Looking at the food he fed to the pigs, he was compelled to stand up and journey home. He could take the scorn. He could even take the shame and humiliation. The young boy returned because there are times when our hunger is so great that we will do nearly anything to appease it.

Notice that when Jesus said, "Blessed are those who hunger and thirst for righteousness, for they will be filled," he was not blessing people who were already filled with goodness. Jesus did not say, "Blessed are those who have been filled yet act like they are still hungry," or "Blessed are those who have all their junk in order." No. "Blessed are those who hunger and thirst," who lack, who hurt, who are obviously empty, who are willing to do whatever it takes to calm the ache within. Jesus was addressing those with wrecked moral lives. So wrecked, in fact, that he associated their pain with starvation.

I spoke with my stepbrother two weeks ago. He has been in prison for the past year. His tone of voice was very sad. He has a lot of time to think about who he is and who he will become. He holds out hope that when he's released in a few years, things will be different. *He* will be different. He wants his little girl back. He hopes his wife will receive him. He is in a place where the hunger for things to be made right again is overwhelming, and to him Jesus says, "Blessed are you who hunger and thirst for righteousness — for right paths, for a right soul, for your life to be remade — for you will be filled."

Only those who are alive know hunger and thirst, and only the dead don't care. All people fail — and fail miserably. At our best, you and I find our souls caught in cycles we wish we could break, and it is then that we prove whether or not we are truly alive. The living do not accept imprisonment. Even after years of confinement, the living will once again rise up and scream at the bars that surround them, "I hate the way my life is being lived, and I need something different."

Angst at our lifestyles is not a sign of failure. It is a sign that our hearts still beat.

Those who hunger and thirst for righteousness — who hobble

along with deep aches, who press on through difficulty, knowing a fire and a meal are waiting — will be blessed by God, for he has the power to fill them.

It may take years of struggle and confession, battle and failure. The places in my life where I struggle with deadly sins are matters of a decade or more of focus, repentance, shame, and grace. I've traveled some long roads simply to lessen the depth of some of my failures and addictions — just to get to a place where I can receive fresh grace and encouragement again. Often, that is how change occurs. The Great Wall of China took centuries to build, and one day your soul and mine will be far more impressive.

Sloth — indifference toward our souls — alone will keep us from the life we are made for. Sloth will praise the ruts we dig, and even when we know they are unhealthy, sloth will tell us this is just the way life is. But it is all a lie. We are made to overflow with life, and Jesus said even those who are utterly starved of goodness have hope, for despite our lack — despite our failures — those who hunger and thirst for righteousness sit at the center of God's desire for us. Though we fail now, it will not always be this way. God is moving you and me from places where our lives are foul into realms of refreshment. He sees our future. He is slowly cutting away the gangrene so we can stand again. He is bandaging up our broken legs so we can run for the first time. But above all, it takes passion to sit again and again on the operating table. It takes passion to care for limbs being reconstructed.

Those who hunger and thirst for righteousness have nothing to hold on to but a promise as they endure surgery. But the promise is beautiful: You will be made whole. The door you are knocking on will be opened. You will be filled, and your fullness will overflow everywhere.

4

GREED AND THE MERCY GIVER

"From everyone who has been given much,
much will be demanded;
and from the one who has been entrusted with much,
much more will be asked."
JESUS OF NAZARETH

My wife and I live in Colorado with our two toddlers. We prefer the outdoors, but when it gets cold, we spend our days playing inside. Until recently, we were unfamiliar with the midday lineup on television. It's a whole new world. The shows all have the same basic premise: beautiful people humiliating themselves. Some of the more popular ones are *Lifestyles of the Rich and Famous* rip-offs: MTV's *Cribs* and VH1's *The Fabulous Life of . . .* Even ESPN has one online. My favorite thing about these shows devoted to pretentious mansions comes near the end, when the camera pulls back for the aerial shot. From above, you don't see majestic foyers or rooms with eight PlayStations. You don't see unused designer cooktops or pools with mosaic self-portraits at the bottom. What you notice are huge fences and lots of palm trees. The homes no longer look like homes. They look like drug lord compounds.

On these shows, the rich and famous build huge bubbles in which to live. Bubbles that shield out the rest of the world. Bubbles that keep them safe. Bubbles that, while beautiful, are really just extravagant fortresses minus the moat. This makes some sense, because celebrities with money probably have a lot of *interesting* people who want to get to know them better. These people may be weird or messy. They may be dangerous. In fact, they may want to steal some of the celebrities' things. But still, it must feel superb to live in a bubble marked with Robin Leach's stamp of approval.

This type of bubble thinking isn't just for the super-rich, either. Look down the street of any new housing development, and sticking out of the front of nearly every home you'll see a garage. A garage allows people like you and me to leave our houses without being infected by our neighbors. In fact, the *real* middle-class bubble isn't the home; it's the automobile. Our cars get us from home to work with a barricade of steel and safety glass protecting us. Cars let us get dry cleaning, lattes, mail, meals, and liquor without leaving a safe place. America is a country of roads, and these roads are populated with car-shaped bubbles announcing our identity to the outside world — outdoorsy, refined, muscular, posh, environmentally conscious. And if the brand and style don't say enough, there's plenty of room on the back for bumper stickers.

Of course, cars are expensive. Payments, insurance, gas, and maintenance may eat half our paycheck — or more. But isn't the sacrifice worth it? We wouldn't want to ride the bus, after all. People who ride public transportation are weird and messy. They may be dangerous. They may want to steal our stuff. And besides, it feels so good to have a leather-upholstered, Bose-equipped, keep-the-rest-of-the-world-out bubble.

As our standard of living increases, the move is toward better, more luxurious bubbles. You and I "move up" into gated communities. We buy thicker, bigger cars with alarms and talking maps so we don't have to ask a real person for directions. We download news and music to occupy our attention. If we are really savvy, our banking, entertainment, and work can all be done from home, in the solitude of our bubbles. I am no different from anyone else here. It seems that everything I purchase and enjoy has been fashioned so I can avoid other people.

This trend is global. In 1998, a year of relative peace, nations around the world spent $780 billion on defense.[1] No less than six million children under the age of five died that year because of a lack of adequate food,[2] and many humanitarian organizations pointed out that if a relatively insignificant portion of that money had been used to benefit the poorest people on earth, the global community could have nearly eliminated global hunger, polluted drinking water, and preventable diseases for many years to come.

Let's be honest. The money we spend on defense isn't about saving lives. Our global priorities are focused on erecting bigger, badder, more intimidating bubbles. We want someone somewhere to know they shouldn't mess with us. We easily affirm the bubble rationale. People out there are weird and messy. They might be dangerous.[3] They may want to steal our stuff, and anyway, living in a country with warplanes that can bomb the opposition without a pilot is pretty stinking sweet. It makes me feel good about my country.

These tendencies of fear, greed, and pride, when multiplied over and over again, create families, societies, and whole kingdoms where the bubble mentality reigns supreme. As we accumulate more and more stuff, it seems as though we're acting out a God-given imperative to build higher, thicker walls. We may even explain to others who drool over our bubbles how much "God has blessed us." Because bubbles make us feel fortunate. They make us feel secure. In many ways, bubbles look out for us and provide the life we want. Over time, they can occupy most of our thoughts and energies, and though we might not say it this way, our bubbles often receive our fullest devotion and sacrifice.

Yet recall a time when you sat back on a summer day with some kids around and you blew bubbles. Bubbles are beautiful. They give the illusion of being strong glass spheres. They tempt us to catch them, to touch them, to hold them as long as we can. But they are temporary. They can't control their own direction. Any passing breeze blows them off course. One book of the Bible begins by asking, "What does anyone gain from all their labors at which they toil under the sun?" And the writer concludes, "All of them are meaningless, a chasing after the wind."[4] This is the benefit of a bigger, better bubble.

Wind.

From empires to everyday fortunes, our bubbles are unreliable. They're erratic. They do not fulfill their promises. And they often separate us from what is truly good. Yet from the beginning, our history as a species has been characterized by the pursuit of the bigger, better bubble. Augustine called this mind-set and the societies it creates "the city of man."[5] It is a futile, self-destructive way of thinking. Hundreds of millions of people have died so that someone somewhere might have a bigger, better, more secure, more impressive bubble.

Certainly we need tools, clothing, and shelter to survive. Certainly God's world is good and ought to be enjoyed. In purchasing a new home, typing on a new computer, or sitting down to a well-prepared meal, many of us experience a God-given happiness. The world around us ought to be seen as a *means* to our bliss. But when we make the created order into an *end* — an idol requiring our devotion — we slip into a form of hell known as *greed*.

Greed is not gluttony, which indulges to the point of bursting.[6]

Greed in many ways couldn't care less about enjoying its spoils. Greed pursues *accumulation*. Greed is the desire to possess more than I need, because of fear or idolatry. A fitting personification of greed is Ebenezer Scrooge, who sat alone at night with a single candle to light his cold bedroom. "Darkness is cheap," wrote Charles Dickens, "and Scrooge liked it."[7]

Scrooge's desire for accumulation may seem like an innocent mistake — an unhealthy love of wealth. But when the greedy spend all their time and talents stashing away gain, what was meant for all is hoarded slowly in the vaults of the few efficient collectors. Greed effectively hardens our hearts; it is fully content to decimate — or leave decimated — the lives of others, as long as a bank account, garage, or pantry with our name on it fills up somewhere.

Unlike the fictional film character Gordon Gekko,[8] who called greed "good" because it "works," the ancient writer Dante depicted the greedy as being chained to the ground, with their backs turned to heaven and their eyes fixed on the earth.[9] The destructive power of greed was noted by one of these shades, who said, "Greed quenched our love of good, thus all our labors were in vain."[10]

Dante rightly sees the problem. Greed is a misdirected love. Like sloth, greed turns our passions from what is actually valuable and hands us mere bubbles that cannot love us in return. Cars, coins, and idols are incapable of receiving or giving affection. One ancient writer said of the bubbles we erect, "They know nothing, they understand nothing; their eyes are plastered over so they cannot see, and their minds closed so they cannot understand."[11] Furthermore, this writer understood that we become like what we worship, and as our bubbles take priority over the everlasting souls around us, we become less and less human.

Though it may be the most socially accepted — even praised — of the deadly sins, the damage greed inflicts on our world is cata-strophic. Jesus' brother James called greed the primary obstacle to peace in our world.[12] Paul wrote that monetary greed is "a root of all kinds of evil."[13] All four gospel writers suggest that Judas betrayed Jesus partially because of greed.[14] At its core, greed prefers wealth to the growth of our soul, to the God who made us, and to peace among people. Thus the greedy trade their humanity for mere bub-bles — each destined to pop.

Tearing Down and Building Up

Greed is a condition of the heart. Greed adores goods that are tem-porary and rejects those that are everlasting. Greed does not care about living well in the present, because greed focuses on the future, and the future is a place of fear — fear that I will not have enough for tomorrow, fear that somehow the God who gives me each breath will stop providing if I do not squirrel away all I can. When speak-ing about greed, Jesus often focused here: "Therefore I tell you, do not worry about your life, what you will eat or drink; or about your body, what you will wear. Is not life more important than food, and the body more important than clothes? Look at the birds of the air; they do not sow or reap or store away in barns, and yet your heavenly Father feeds them. Are you not much more valuable than they?"[15]

Jesus spoke about greed more than any other sin. He consistently addressed the human desire to possess and hoard, to place hope in fleeting resources and not in the God of heaven. Jesus even said that the affluent — those who have not shared what God has given them with the desperately impoverished — are a wretched lot.[16]

Nearing the end of his life, Jesus addressed a crowd that was "trampling on one another,"[17] asking him to resolve all kinds of disputes over money: "Watch out! Be on your guard against all kinds of greed; *life* does not consist in an abundance of possessions."[18]

The New Testament uses the Greek words *bios* and *zōē* to describe "life."[19] *Bios* is biological life. It is the life of plants and animals. *Zōē* is the deeper kind of life. It does not consist of breathing or a heartbeat. It is your soul life. It's the life God breathes into you. Jesus used the latter term here and said, in effect, "Watch out! If you give yourself to greed, you may lose your soul life." To illustrate the point, Jesus then told this story:

> "The ground of a certain rich man yielded an abundant harvest. He thought to himself, 'What shall I do? I have no place to store my crops.'
>
> "Then he said, 'This is what I'll do. I will tear down my barns and build bigger ones, and there I will store my surplus grain. And I'll say to myself, "You have plenty of grain laid up for many years. Take life easy; eat, drink and be merry." '
>
> "But God said to him, 'You fool! This very night your life will be demanded from you. Then who will get what you have prepared for yourself?'
>
> "This is how it will be with those who store up things for themselves but are not rich toward God."[20]

Jesus described two moral failures here. Not only did the rich man hoard his crop, but once the rich man "had his," he *could* have spent the rest of his life working for the benefit of the destitute. Instead, he decided to move to Florida and play golf for the rest of his days. He did not use his land or his skills to benefit the hungry. His wealth and his crop were restricted to his own bubble, and he left his land to fill up with weeds.[21]

Both failures result from the rich man's obliviousness to the plight of the poor around him. When he asks, "What shall I do?" he is unaware that a small sacrifice could improve the lives of scores of people, especially in first-century Palestine, which certainly had its share of hunger. His sin was both a failure to act *and* a failure to know.

This isn't a story just for another time. We likewise fail to know where the world is hurting and to act on our knowledge. It happened to me recently. I came across a statistic indicating that nearly 18,000 kids today will die simply because they are malnourished.[22] That's about six times the number of human beings killed on September 11 — every day. That works out to over 125,000 children each week, a far faster clip than even the Holocaust.

Why isn't this more front and center in my discussions? Why am I more concerned with how I am going to fund my 401(k) than with the destitute in my world? One report I read flatly assumed ambivalence like mine and said of these kids, "They die quietly in some of the poorest villages on earth, far removed from the scrutiny and the conscience of the world."[23]

Many of us in wealthier nations don't just fail to solve these problems; we fail even to *look* for these problems. Our newscasts our filled with women who shave their heads, celebrities going to prison, child custody disputes between the rich and the dead, and all the political horse racing you could wish for. Showing emaciated children on the front page every day may not sell many newspapers, but it seems we don't even know such horrors exist.[24]

When the rich man in Jesus' story began to consider what he would do with his newfound fortune, he seemed oblivious as well. Notice the person he consulted. *The Message* reads, "He talked to himself: ... Then he said, 'Here's what I'll do: ... I'll gather in all my grain and goods, and I'll say to myself, "Self, you've done well! You've got it made and can now retire. Take it easy and have the time of your life!"'" The man consulted no one else. His greed had ostracized him from everyone else, and as I have said before, if you are alone in one of Jesus' stories, your life is a picture of hell.

I suspect most of us don't need a large windfall like the rich man's to be guilty of ignoring the needs around us. We each could sacrifice one significant thing to save someone's life. Take nearly any category of consumer goods you and I buy for pleasure — perfume, DVDs, lattes, books on Jesus' teachings. The money Americans spend on each of these categories could eliminate the most devastating problems our world faces. For example, Americans spend somewhere around $41 billion a year on their pets.[25] Economist Jeffery Sachs led a commission several years ago that estimated the annual cost to create basic disease control and health systems for the world's poor at $30 billion a year.[26] I'm not suggesting you should starve your Labrador for the sake of the impoverished, but imagine if each of us set aside $20 each time we bought a bag of dog food. That alone could *radically* transform our planet.

The problem of desperate poverty is far from insurmountable. Among other things, the world needs a grassroots movement of common generosity. It needs aware, informed individuals and families everywhere to tear down our current picture of the good life and erect a new one in its place.[27]

When the rich man in Jesus' story said, "I will *tear down* my barns and build bigger ones," he used an epic phrase found in Jeremiah.[28] The prophet Jeremiah used this phrase to describe courageous acts, but in an ironic twist, Jesus put these words in the mouth of the rich man.[29] It's as though storing up treasures to enjoy tomorrow is the complete opposite of a good and courageous act, and God calls the rich man a "fool" — a man with nothing good inside him. And God took the man's life back as though he were already dead.

What we tear down and rebuild says everything about our souls, our future, and the things we really value. We can tear down our current lifestyle and rebuild a new one filled with generosity, or we can tear down barns that have kept us more than comfortable and erect newer, bigger ones to replace them. Often you and I may look at the wealth we have accumulated and say to ourselves, "Self, what shall I do with all this?" And all too often our answer is an updated iPod, a newer automobile, a flatter television set — just another meaningless bubble.

Conversely, Jesus taught that if you have the necessary skills and resources, it is a good thing to make all the money you can, to fill your fields with crops, *and then to give as much of it away as possible.*[30] We should not neglect the former or the latter. Every breath we receive is a gift from God. How much more the overabundance in our hands? Excess is not given for us to hoard; excess is given that we may become extravagant gift givers — just like God is. Each little bit of extra that falls into our laps is an opportunity to become more Godlike.

In this way, the merciful reflect their Creator. They become what they were always meant to be. The greedy, however, show themselves devoid of such life, lacking the only thing that matters. As Jesus said, "What good will it be for you to gain the whole world, yet forfeit your soul?"[31]

The Neglected Art of Breathing

Receiving and giving away characterize the basic motion of life. A constant in-and-out exchange animates both plant and animal life.

Obviously, a failure to inhale is fatal, but so is a refusal to exhale. If the air we draw in is not released, carbon dioxide will build in our blood and the body's internal oxygen level will drop; and if we continue to hold our breath, brain damage and death will soon follow. Those who fill their lungs without releasing the air perish in the same way as those whose lungs are empty.

The same is true of God's mercy.

Twice Jesus was questioned about receiving God's mercy — once by a legal scholar and once by a rich ruler. Both asked the same question: "What must I do to inherit eternal life?"[32] That is, what is required for God to show *me* mercy? Both men wanted to justify their lifestyles to themselves. Both men were given much, and as it turns out, both men were suffocating on what they had been given.

To the rich ruler, Jesus simply said, "You still lack one thing. Sell everything you have and give to the poor, and you will have treasure in heaven. Then come, follow me."[33] When the young man heard Jesus' response, he became sad and turned away. The answer exposed his cloven heart — torn between the desire for God's kind of life and the riches of a world filled with holes.[34] The man had come to Jesus wanting life. He wanted the God kind of life, the eternal kind of life. He wanted *zōē*, and so Jesus told him that he needed to breathe:

> "Sell everything ..." (Exhale.)
> "Then come, follow me." (Inhale.)
> "Sell everything ..." (Exhale.)
> "Then come, follow me." (Inhale.)

Jesus would not leave the man with nothing. Jesus would give him the only kind of life worth having.

The rich ruler declined, and as he walked away, Jesus said to his

followers, "How hard it is for the rich to enter the kingdom of God!"[35]
Not because acquiring wealth is bad (in fact, as we saw above, one
of the moral failures of the rich fool was that he quit working), but
because the rich — as in this case — have chosen not to limit their
fears and needs and bank accounts for the sake of others. Again, in
the teachings of Jesus, there is a moral imperative both to make all
you can and to simply release it like a breath.

Earlier in Jesus' travels, a scholar of religious law had also asked
Jesus how to obtain God's mercy.[36] The man knew the answer: Love
God, and love your neighbor. It was clear from the Scriptures. But
the scholar pressed Jesus to tell him exactly whom he ought to consider a neighbor. The scholar may have heard Jesus' other stories; he
may have caught the flow of Jesus' other teachings that embraced
the pagans, rejected the land, rejected the temple, rejected even the
exclusive redemption of the Jewish people. By asking this question,
the scholar thought he had given Jesus enough rope to hang himself
before the crowd. Familiar with Jesus' teachings, the scholar knew
Jesus would respond, "Everyone is your neighbor," a radically unacceptable answer to be sure. Such an answer would have rejected
a common understanding of the Torah. This scholar felt comfortable leading Jesus here, we may assume, because the scholar's peers
wouldn't favor such an answer; neither would the crowd, and of
course neither would he. The scholar had just set Jesus up, and he
would leave justified, loving only those he chose to.

But Jesus told the man a fresh story about breathing out.

Once upon a time, Jesus began, a man was traveling the road
between the holy city and a resort town when he was beaten and
stripped by a gang of robbers who left the man half dead. This road
was well traveled by those approaching the holy city, and soon a
priest came by and saw the beaten man lying in the road. The priest

paused. "If this bloody man dies in my arms," he thought, "I will be ceremonially unclean and unable to do my priestly duties." So the priest passed by the man, looking ahead to the holy city. Just then a religious man approached the blood-soaked body. Not wanting to miss any of the festivities himself, he also avoided the body. But then a fascist Iranian trial lawyer passed by (at least that's close to what Jesus' contemporaries may have heard when he said "Samaritan"). Filled with pity, the Samaritan reached into his bag, stooped down, and poured the holy items he had reserved for himself on the man's wounds. He then took the broken man to a place of rest. "When I return," the Samaritan said to the innkeeper, "I will make everything right again." And he left the man in good care.[37]

The scholar, like most of his contemporaries, hated the Samaritan half-breeds,[38] so when Jesus asked which of the three men in his story was a neighbor to the half-dead traveler, the scholar did not say, "The Samaritan." He replied with proper academic detachment, "The one who had mercy on him."[39]

Jesus responded that if you desire God's mercy — if you want God to breathe into your life — then "go and do likewise." Go and breathe on others. Take in the good things God gives you, and give them away.

In many of his parables, Jesus taught that those who hoard God's mercy die.[40] Like a person breathing in and persistently refusing to exhale, those who stockpile the gifts of God are destroyed by them. Both the rich ruler and the scholar had trouble breathing out the mercy God had shown them, and therefore both men had difficulty understanding and receiving God's eternal kind of life.

Jesus' hard teaching that it is nearly impossible for the rich to enter the kingdom of heaven is worth meditating on. The priest and the religious man in the story of the good Samaritan were greedy. They hoarded what was given to heal. They used what God entrusted to them for personal benefit alone. In short, they chose to breathe mercy in but not to breathe it out again. Perhaps it is difficult for the rich to enter the kingdom of heaven — not because acquiring wealth is bad, but because wealth, like air, provides not only what we need to live but also the power to purge the toxins of greed, fear, and self-reliance as we release it. If we do not breathe such poisons out, we will surely suffocate on them.

In contrast to the priest and the religious man, the good Samaritan was a mercy giver, and by giving mercy he reflected the life of God. Early Christian and medieval writers noted that the parable of the good Samaritan parallels the story of Jesus' redeeming the world.[41] Humankind has been beaten down by sin, left for dead, and stripped of all that was once good. Yet neither our religious duties (the priest) nor the law of God (the religious man, the Levite) can save us, but a foreigner — a different kind of man from a different kind of world, in fact — can. Jesus saw our condition and had mercy on us. Stooping down to a dark place, he poured wine (his blood) and oil (his Spirit) on our wounds. Then he brought us to a place where others (the church, perhaps) would care for us. And when Jesus left, he promised those listening that he would return someday and make everything right again.

God is a breathing God. In his mercy for us, the Father gave his Son; the Son gave his life. God exhaled mercy into a sin-drenched world, and when he inhaled again, his breath — the Spirit — collected all who would receive his mercy. In and out. God does not hoard but gives freely; and when he gives, God receives. Giving away and receiving mark the kind of life going on inside of God. It is what he is about. Giving away and therefore receiving is the eternal kind of life.

In one of his letters, the apostle Paul makes a list of all the things that he once thought made him alive and godly: his education, his heritage, his spotless record.[42] Then he pauses. And he calls it — all of it — excrement. It may be the most beautiful piece of writing in the Scriptures. The only thing worthy of his boasting, writes Paul, is the mercy Jesus gave him when he was picked up in his own half-dead condition, lungs filled with venom,[43] on his own road between the holy city and Damascus.

What must we do to inherit the eternal kind of life? As Adam — a pile of dust — breathed in the breath of God and so became a living being, and as Jesus breathed on his disciples and said, "Receive the Holy Spirit,"[44] so too we must empty our lungs as much as we are able in order to receive God's life-giving breath.[45] Like the rich ruler, we cannot have it both ways. We must begin to give away the life we have in order to receive the only life worth having.

Thus Paul exhorts his listeners, in view of the mercy God breathes out, to take their ordinary lives and give them to God as an offering. This, says Paul, is the only appropriate response to God's love.[46] Nothing less. In the same fashion, Jesus said, "Whoever wants to save their life will lose it, but whoever loses their life for me and for the gospel will save it."[47] Life in Christ is all about breathing. Forgive and you will be forgiven. Love as I have loved you. Do to others what you would have them do to you. Be humbled and you will be exalted. Give and you will receive.

Most crucial of all, in the Beatitudes, Jesus said, "Blessed are the merciful, for they will be shown mercy." The merciful alone — those who extend the gifts of God to others — will see and receive God's mercy.

STAGNANT PONDS

Viktor Frankl, a psychiatrist and Holocaust survivor, said of his experience at Auschwitz that those who gave away food were more likely to survive. He described a common scene during his time in the concentration camps. Most mornings in the barracks, a man would simply choose not to get up again. Though not yet dead, he would lay motionless on his bunk for days — giving up on hope, giving up on meaning — until what Frankl said was a frequent final act. The dying man would pull out a cigarette from his urine- and excrement-soaked straw bed, smoke it, and then die.

The scene was frequent and tragic. Frankl often asked himself how he and his fellow inmates could possibly avoid the same fate.

At the climax to his book, Frankl tells the story of a man, starved and desperate, who stole some potatoes from the Nazi kitchen. The guards found out and announced that all twenty-five hundred men in the camp would go without food the next day if the thief was not handed over immediately.

All twenty-five hundred men chose to fast.

After a day without the normal miniscule rations, the men grumbled in their bunks that night, short-tempered and miserable. But then some began to rise and speak. They reaffirmed to the group the meaning found in being merciful. Sacrifices, one noted, often appear pointless in the material world of success, but here sacrifice had saved a living human being from a tragic end. Even if the sacrifice resulted in their own death, one man said, it would show that they were alive in the only way that mattered. These twenty-five hundred men would not die stripped of everything, lying on mats of filth with only a last cigarette to comfort them. They would experience the giving and sharing of life, and that alone gave the inmates something to live for.[48]

Frankl, one of the twentieth century's greatest psychologists, said it was this sense of meaning and purpose that drove the men forward, that kept them from dying without hope. Saving that one man was the purpose they would have otherwise lacked in the cold, monotonous death camps. It propelled them forward. Many of these men who went hungry that day were rescued by Allied forces just a few weeks later.

God's mercy is not dualistic, focusing on a person's soul and discarding the body. When Jesus announced the inbreaking of God's kingdom, he first healed the sick and fed the hungry. This was the only sign necessary for his audience to understand that everything was different. God was changing the world.

To the religious elite who took in God's mercy but gave none of it away, Jesus told a story of men who were given charge of a vineyard and who hoarded its fruit for themselves.[49] When the vineyard owner sent his son to collect some of the fruit, the tenants killed the son and threw his body out of the vineyard. "What then will the owner of the vineyard do?" Jesus asked the religious elite. "He will come and kill those tenants and give the vineyard to others."[50] The religious elite of Jesus' day hoarded God's mercy while the surrounding country starved, and Jesus spoke of their demise with the harshest words imaginable: The task you have been given will be taken from you and given to someone else, and you will be tossed aside like so much trash.

A church that chooses to build bigger bubbles for itself (individually and collectively) while the world starves does not participate in the spreading of God's kingdom. Christians in the affluent West who relish the fact that "God has blessed us" ought to remember that the same God has cast aside a self-described chosen people before.

Conversely, Jesus taught us the proper place for our wealth: "From everyone who has been given much, much will be demanded."[51] "It is more blessed to give than to receive."[52] "Freely you have received, freely give."[53] Giving mercy not only reaffirms the humanity of others; it reaffirms and invigorates our own humanity. Even in the most desperate places, those who give away what they have are the ones who in the end truly receive. By exhaling, they inhale all that really matters.

The merciful alone, said Jesus, will be shown God's mercy. The rest will suffocate in the irrelevant bubbles they blow.

5

LUST AND
THE PURE OF HEART

All that we are is dependent on our thoughts.
It begins with our thoughts,
it continues with our thoughts,
it ends with our thoughts.
THE BUDDHA

DAN WAS A YOUTH WORKER RESPONSIBLE FOR 150 MIDDLE SCHOOL students. He couldn't do it alone, so he had a few paid helpers and volunteers who worked with him. One of his volunteers — we'll call him Greg — had been Dan's roommate. He was in Dan's wedding. He seemed like a fully trustworthy and capable guy. Last year, Greg was arrested for seducing one of the thirteen-year-old girls in Dan's youth group. A few days after the arrest, Dan visited Greg in prison. "Man, how did this happen?" he asked. "How did you make such a massive leap and do something like that?" Greg told Dan that it wasn't a jump at all. It was just another small step.

Greg had tried to live a normal life in front of his peers. He worked hard to keep himself together, but Greg had some real issues. He had always felt insecure around women. He didn't have the confidence to woo and win a girl's affection, so he began turning to pornography. Porn was an easy way for him to appease his desires without making himself vulnerable to another human being. That was a basic step for Greg. It wasn't a huge leap. It is a step a lot of people take in their private lives. After some time, Greg began to take other steps. He began spending more and more time and money consuming porn. Soon he began frequenting strip clubs, which was just another step beyond his rampant use of pornography. After learning how the clubs worked, he began to pay for lap dances. He began paying for more explicit favors. He grew accustomed to actual women serving his sexual needs on demand. Over time, it simply became his way of life.

And one day — after a few years of viewing thousands of pictures, after actively giving control of his body and his mind to lust over and over again — he took another small step and used just another girl. But this step destroyed his life.

Now he lives in prison. When he leaves, he will have to register as a pedophile wherever he goes. Now he's so ashamed of his past, he no longer speaks with those who once cared about him. These steps — made in his private life — ultimately destroyed him.

In our culture, brokenness birthed from misguided sexual pursuits is widespread. The value placed on sexual indulgence leads many to destroy their families, squander their savings, and even give up on life itself. It is certainly healthy to want sex. There even are profound truths that can be discovered through sex. However, when our desire for sex takes over — when our appetites demand whatever they wish without commitment or care — our sexual longings step beyond their natural role. The sexual passions make wonderful servants but terrible masters, and when given authority, their rule is untamed.

We call such rule by our primal urges *lust*. Lust is handing control of my body and mind over to illicit cravings. Those controlled by lust know something is wrong inside them, for they make their habits private. They hide evidence from those they care about most. Shame often reveals not just where we mess up but where our lives malfunction.

Yet if you are like me, such breakdowns could be rampant. I often think Darwinism gets its widespread popularity not from fossils or finch beaks, but because it explains why we are so consumed with sex. Our bodies yearn for sex, real or imagined. A reckless sexual craving seems built into our DNA. But we must be sure to put such longings in their place and not allow them to rule us.

Imagine we have visited an alien world where scores of people assemble to watch a striptease. Imagine, however, that instead of a woman, a small, covered platter is brought out, and with all eyes wide, someone slowly removes the lid, revealing a steaming hamburger. We think this "striptease" is a joke, but all around us, people begin howling. Others snicker, elbowing their friends. Some just sit quivering in their seats.[1] If such a world did exist, we would think this display not merely odd; we would think something inside the audience was broken. A healthy appetite for food is good, but when appetites turn into manic behavior, something is in a state of disrepair.

Just so, not everything our bodies want is healthy. Good health requires our organs to function in precise ways and at precise times. The heart, kidneys, and liver have detailed roles, tasks they are supposed to do. When the heart pumps blood too slowly to the body or when the kidneys fail to clean debris from our blood, we rightly say these organs are not working properly. Why not think the same of our desires? Why place them in a different category? Shouldn't our desires aim at health-producing targets? Shouldn't our desires make our minds and bodies and even our souls healthier?

Lust has the opposite effect.

Like all extremes, an out-of-control desire for sex is damaging. When we give lust the steering wheel, it will rot our normal desire for sex, making it hollow and unappeasable. We can talk sensibly about brain damage. We may even say that a certain man is a lunatic, that his mind is erratic and unstable. In the same way, lust, if given its way, will make our bodies and minds erratic and unstable. When we give control of our lives over to lust, we lose not only the potential joy of sex but also the enjoyment of so much else. At its core, lust wars against the community we ought to share with one another — distorting duties, confusing friendships, breaking up marriages, betraying children, creating false intimacy, turning us away from the pleasure of another person toward mere self-gratification. As one ancient confession reads, "With the lusts of passion I have darkened the beauty of my soul, and turned my whole mind entirely to dust."[2]

Broken sexuality, however, is not always lust. We may note that unhealthy sexuality is an expression of each of the other deadly sins. Often sexual dysfunction is a form of greed, wanting more and more images or more and more partners. In like manner, a sex glutton will fill his life with sexual experiences to the point where his mind and body break down. More common still is the husband who, because of sloth, does not pursue his wife by sacrificing for her, loving her in creative ways, giving his best energy to her, and so finding her worthy of his love. Instead, he turns to adult websites to unenthusiastically appease himself.

So too, others may experience sloth in sexuality by not engaging their partner at all. They may suffer from pride — using sex to control and manipulate another or seeking to show ownership of a partner through sexual denial or demand. Even more tragic, some may begin to hate themselves through sex, either giving themselves to multiple partners in self-loathing or torturing themselves through starvation and the like because they find their bodies inadequate. Wrath aimed at oneself is perhaps the most tragic example of broken sexuality.

Both genders seem to experience envy for other sexual partners. Yet sexual dysfunction is most often associated with lust. Lust can produce a deep pleasure and often comes to mind first when we think of "sin."

The early church fathers judged lust not by its euphoric fruit but by its destructive tendencies. These men were not prudes, and still they never shied away from saying that lust contributes to human misery. They could have affirmed unrestrained sexuality as a gift from the Creator. Instead, they saw lust as a thief and a deceiver, overwhelming the mind and pointing it toward illusions, with no real ability to grant what they offer. They spoke of lust as filler for the empty soul. Aquinas wrote, "Man cannot live without joy; therefore when he is deprived of true spiritual joys it is necessary that he become addicted to carnal pleasures."[3]

Early Christians — most lasting religious traditions, in fact — objected to lust not because it produces ecstasy but because the ecstasy produced is a third-rate substitute for something real. Lust turns us from the hope of long-lasting bliss and offers us vapor, for we were not made to be mere animals who procreate and die. We are made to be so much more. Even if an evolutionary process produced humanity, God has created us for one more great leap out of the animal whims that birthed us and into the kind of life and happiness he experiences.

Yet lust offers us a wasteland of broken relationships and illusory pleasures instead.

A VALLEY OF BURNING WASTE

When Jesus spoke of sin, he often chose to address greed, hypocrisy, and pride first. Lust for him was neither the most powerful nor the most lethal of the sins. Perhaps this is why he said the prostitutes were entering the kingdom of God ahead of the Pharisees.[4] Sins of the flesh are bad, but those that darken the soul are terminal. This isn't to gloss over the destructive power of lust, only to set it in its correct place. Lust is not the worst sin, only the most popular.[5] Still, Jesus says something striking about our misplaced sexual urges:

> "You have heard that it was said, 'You shall not commit adultery.' But I tell you that anyone who looks at [another person] lustfully has already committed adultery ... in [their] heart. If your right eye causes you to stumble, gouge it out and throw it away. It is better for you to lose one part of your body than for your whole body to be thrown into hell. And if your right hand causes you to stumble, cut it off and throw it away. It is better for you to lose one part of your body than for your whole body to go into hell."[6]

I find this the single most difficult passage in the New Testament. It's extreme. It's piercing. And it sits right in the middle of the most important sermon Jesus gave on how we ought to live. If you want to know what Jesus said about the health of our sexual lives, here it is — and repeated for emphasis is the encouragement to amputate a body part.

At the very least, we can say that Jesus took lust seriously, even if it wasn't at the top of his list. Pulling out a cleaver and hacking off pieces of flesh is a fairly radical prescription. Yet if we want to honor the entirety of Jesus' teaching, this passage is unavoidable. Perhaps if we look again, we'll find more than radical surgery. In order to get there, however, we need to know something about the history of the world in which Jesus walked, to which he spoke, and from which he drew his illustrations.

Around the year 735 BC, King Ahaz of Judah — and later his grandson Manasseh — took over the great temple of the Lord and used it to worship a pagan god called Baal.[7] In the Bible, Baal often refers to fertility gods who many believed brought the rain. As a desert people, the Israelites found leaving God to worship the Baals to be a regular temptation in two ways. First, worship often entailed having sex with temple prostitutes, and second, many Israelites found it difficult to pray for rain and wait on their God's grace when the simple act of engaging in a few rituals at a pagan temple down the road held the promise of feeding the whole family. The twofold combination of illicit sex and daily bread was enough to draw many away from God over the years.

More tragic still, the Baals weren't content with small displays of devotion. Just beyond the city walls of Jerusalem lay a canyon known as the Valley of Ben Hinnom. Pagans of this period would create large fire pits there, and as an act of worship they would burn children alive. In response, the prophet Jeremiah said to the people of Judah:

"'So shave your heads.
   Go bald to the hills and lament,
For GOD has rejected and left
   this generation that has made him so angry.'

"The people of Judah have lived evil lives while I've stood by and watched." GOD's Decree. "In deliberate insult to me, they've set up their obscene god-images in the very Temple that was built to honor me. They've constructed Topheth altars for burning babies in prominent places all through the valley of Ben-hinnom, altars for burning their sons and daughters alive in the fire — a shocking perversion of all that I am and all I command.

"But soon, very soon" — GOD's Decree! — "the names Topheth and Ben-hinnom will no longer be used. They'll call the place what it is: Murder Meadow.[8] Corpses will be stacked up in Topheth because there's no room left to bury them! Corpses abandoned in the open air, fed on by crows and coyotes, who have the run of the place."[9]

And so it came to pass. In the year 586 BC, armies from Babylon entered Judah.[10] Parked outside the gates of Jerusalem for two years, the Babylonians starved the people inside. When they finally broke through, they destroyed the Jewish temple and set the city on fire. The Babylonians captured the king of Judah[11] — the last descendant of David to reign in Israel. They killed the king's sons in front of him, then cut out his eyes and carted him to Babylon in chains. After all the bloodshed, the bodies of the slain Hebrews — many of whom had rejected God for Baal — were thrown in the Valley of Ben Hinnom, the same valley where their children had been murdered and their evil practices conducted for the last century.

By Jesus' day, the name of this valley was shortened to Gehenna.[12] Gehenna served as the local dump. All the city's waste and debris were burned there. Executed criminals and unburied bodies were often thrown into Gehenna, giving the chasm its reputation as the place of the damned and the forsaken. The fires of the valley created a stench that colored the whole area. Those in the city could see its smoke, and the pollution was a reminder to all of past disgrace.

In Jesus' mind, Gehenna was a place of faithlessness, where those called to be something great had turned their backs on God. At Gehenna, rebellious Hebrews had sacrificed their children to the fires of Baal. At Gehenna, foreign armies had piled thousands of corpses as the surviving Israelites were led into exile. Gehenna was quite literally a place of burning bodies and smoldering waste — which brings a lot of clarity to what Jesus said about our sexual lives. When Jesus said it's better to remove an eye or hand to avoid "hell," the word used was *Gehenna*.[13]

There are real consequences to lust, and Jesus peeled off a scab from Israel's past to illustrate them. Jesus was saying that when we lust, we are throwing our whole selves into a valley of burning waste — a place of death and idolatry and rejectedness and smoldering trash.

Thus, Jesus taught that Gehenna is so awful that a wise person would gladly trade an eye to avoid diving into its heat. Jesus' statement was a pragmatic observation. It's like saying it is better to starve for a month than eat poisoned meat. He insisted that if you cannot keep your eyes or hands in check, then you must make a choice between bad and terrible — between self-mutilation and total ruin. Jesus' teaching was not concerned with good and bad. Dismemberment is never a *good* thing. The choice here is between horrific and soul destroying.

Perhaps we should ask whether there are any other possibilities. Perhaps we can avoid both fire and amputation, *and that is precisely the point.* Jesus aimed not to produce more sockets and stumps but to illustrate the vile weight of lust. Jesus certainly knew that plucking an eye from one's skull or sawing off a hand is a grotesque matter. He wanted to awaken passions of a different sort, to show where our thought life leads if it is not radically addressed. He called us to take back control from soul-destroying lust. Amputation is just one potential remedy.[14] Certainly we are smart enough to think of others that don't result in bloodshed.

Seeking the Face of God

Lustful urges can be impossible to quench once ignited. Lust is like an all-consuming cloud — a place where our frame of mind is smothered by a furnace of unrealistic fantasies. Most of us can relate to the flames of lust and to the image of trash, and so Gehenna is an appropriate pricture. But we shouldn't think of hell simply as a location somewhere.[15] Hell is above all else an absence of reality.

Jesus saw hell as the darkness outside,[16] the state of being destroyed,[17] the experience of those who perish.[18] We ought to associate sin (the power) and evil (the description) with hell (the condition), perhaps considering them one and the same. The life of hell — if it can even be called that at all — is life decaying until nothing remains.[19] God creates neither sin nor evil nor hell. They exist as the absence of what ought to be.

Hell is where fantasy reigns. Its only substance is illusion. Joy, wonder, and beauty have no place there. Hell is the sphere in which all traces of the life we were made for disappear. Sin encourages us to create a world of our own making. The unfortunate problem is that such a realm cannot exist. Unplugging ourselves from our relationship to reality is not a step into self-legitimacy; it is a step into the abyss, a move toward disintegration.

Conversely, God creates real experiences — real joy, real beauty, and lasting life. When we speak of heaven and hell, this is where we should begin. As C. S. Lewis wrote, "Heaven is reality itself. All that is fully real is Heavenly."[20] The life of heaven is all there really is. Heaven is not a location. Heaven is the sphere of God's reign. Everything that is real moves by the influence and wisdom of God, participating in the one, ultimate heavenly reality.

Because he is the maker and foundation of reality, God has designed us in a certain way. As we study our blueprint, we see that it is in a consistent experience of God that humanity thrives and finds its bliss. God is the fuel our souls require. He is the food we were made to eat. Many of Jesus' own words play this out as he refers to himself as "real food" and "real drink."[21] We are invited to "take and eat."[22] The psalmist calls us to "taste and see that the LORD is good."[23] God made us to feed on the life that he provides. It is not imaginary sustenance. In fact, it is so real that our stomachs often are not prepared for it.

Yet if separated, we starve. Separated, we are left to feed on phantom foods that tickle our appetites but have no meaningful substance. Lust offers just such a meal. The choice is between what is real and what is illusion, between joy and evanescence, between the life we were made for and the life of disoriented craving. These two sets are incompatible. One cannot live within both the real and the imaginary. One cannot feed on both bliss and the carnal. Jesus longed for us to see the horror of Gehenna. Hell is the sphere where God is not — not active, not seen, not enjoyed — nowhere to be found. In hell, we cannot see God.

This is vital to understand, for even from a distance, seeing God is a sign of hope and a promise of life. By seeing God, we feast on what we actually hunger for. By seeing God, we know what our souls require and what is the true appeasement for our deepest longing.

One of the oldest prayers on earth is called the Aaronic benediction. It has been prayed over the Jewish people for nearly four thousand years:

> The LORD bless you
>   and keep you;
> the LORD make his face shine on you
>   and be gracious to you;
> the LORD turn his face toward you
>   and give you peace.[24]

Throughout the Scriptures, the *sight* of God is the supreme end for which we were made. It is the primary attribute of Eden. Seeing God is the great desire of the Hebrew poets. Being near God is an essential description of Jesus' incarnation, and it is the only relevant promise of the life to come. This is what we are made for: to be with God, to walk with him, and to enjoy his company and his presence. In fact, a lengthy book of the Bible is dedicated to the pursuit of God's face.

The book of Job is not so much about suffering as it is about a man who longs desperately to speak to God. Job wants to step into God's presence, defend himself, and ask God questions about his pain and circumstances. At one point, Job says, "I know that my redeemer lives, and that in the end he will stand on the earth. And after my skin has been destroyed, yet in my flesh I will see God; I myself will see him with my own eyes.... *How my heart yearns within me!*"[25] Desire! The book of Job is about one man's fervent passion to see God. The book, in fact, ends with precisely that: God speaking to Job, showing who he is and all he has made.[26]

Everywhere you look in the Scriptures, you will find this longing to see God. In fact, the very last chapter of the Bible shows this desire realized. Revelation pictures a restored world in which heaven has fully engulfed the earth. God has placed his throne here, and it says of those who love him that they will gaze on the face of God.[27] This idea of looking on God is known in literature as the beatific vision. *Beatific* comes from the same Latin word as *beatitude*, meaning "happiness." Over and over again, our experiences and our tradition say that to behold God is bliss. As the psalmist wrote,

> One thing I ask from the LORD,
>   this only do I seek:
> that I may dwell in the house of the LORD
>   all the days of my life,
> to gaze on the beauty of the LORD
>   and to seek him in his temple.[28]

This is just one of many examples, and it seems central to Jesus' understanding of heaven. When Jesus told us in the Beatitudes who is really happy, he promised the beatific vision: *"Blessed are the pure in heart, for they will see God."*

Those who are supremely fortunate are the ones whose hearts are clean, who have a beautiful innocence — for they have the ability to look on God.

THE DESIRE FOR HEAVEN OR HELL

Have you seen God lately?

I haven't either.

We're not very pure, I suppose. I'm not even sure what would happen if we saw God. Would we have a secret kind of vision ("Oh, there he is, walking with the pope")? Should we expect a bush to ignite before us and begin speaking to us? Should we look heavenward? Assuming we were pure enough, would we see shapes in the clouds and hear voices from the sky? These don't seem quite right — or very desirable, for that matter. But how else do we make sense of this beatitude?

Often the New Testament calls those who follow Jesus "temples of the Holy Spirit"[29] or the "temple of God."[30] The idea is that God no longer dwells in buildings of brick and stone. He occupies the hearts of those who love him, especially when they gather together. This is a huge theme in the New Testament. All of us who love Jesus and make him our director, teacher, and savior have God's Spirit remaking us within.

If this is true, then if we were to put on the right sort of glasses, if we had the right kind of perspective, if we saw those around us as vessels (or potential vessels) of God's Spirit instead of mere people, *we would, in fact, see God.* If God actually occupies those who love him — if he populates their praises, works to make them more like himself, breathes through them to restore the world — how can we avoid seeing God if we simply look for him with the right kind of heart?[31] At a masquerade it often takes just a bit of wit and the right desire to deduce the identities of those behind the masks, but those who focus only on the masks go about deceived.

In the same way, many things get in the way of our ability to see God in others. We might say, "I don't care if God is working in that person, because he's kind of repulsive. He's too ugly, too poor, too dumb, too gay, too old, too brown, has just done too many terrible things." On the other hand, we might make an equal and opposite mistake. We might say, "I don't care to see God in that person because I prefer to see something else. I want to use her as a means to satisfy my urges. I want her to make me feel good. I want to burn within, despite the illusion, despite the effect on myself, on my soul, on my world — despite the step over the edge."

I desire Gehenna over Joy.

And this is the crux. *It's all about our desires* — our desire for total happiness that comes in seeing God set against our desire to dive into seething waste.

At the beginning of this chapter, we looked at a passage in which Jesus says, "I tell you that anyone who looks at a [person] *lustfully* has already committed adultery with [them]."[32] There's no word for "lust" in Greek, so the writer uses the words *epithymeō* and *epithymia* — words that denote a deep craving of the heart. But lest we think strong desires are bad, Jesus said at his last supper with his disciples, "I have eagerly desired [*epithymia epethymēsa*] to eat this Passover with you."[33] Paul said in his first letter to Timothy that aspiring — *epithymeō* — to lead in the church is honorable and good,[34] and in another letter Paul said he has a great desire — *epithymia* — to be with Jesus following his death.[35]

One of the reasons Buddhists get it wrong — one of the reasons a lot of Christians get it wrong, for that matter — is they believe we need to get rid of desire. This is not where the Bible stands. We are not Platonists and certainly not Gnostics.[36] The Bible never asks us to purge our desires, as though desire were a bad thing. The biblical encouragement is always to direct the desires we have toward that which is good. Justice. Mercy. Love. Joy. Peace. The fair beauty of the Lord. As C. S. Lewis writes:

> We are told to deny ourselves and to take up our crosses in order that we may follow Christ; and nearly every description of what we shall ultimately find if we do so contains an appeal to desire.... If we consider the unblushing promises of reward and the staggering nature of the rewards promised in the Gospels, it would seem that our Lord finds our desires, not too strong, but too weak. We are half-hearted creatures, fooling about with drink and sex and ambition when infinite joy is offered us, like an ignorant child who wants to go on making mud pies in a slum because he cannot imagine what is meant by the offer of a holiday at sea. We are far too easily pleased.[37]

Lewis unpacks this idea further in his book *The Great Divorce*, which features a man standing between heaven and hell with a little red lizard on his shoulder.[38] The lizard's words captivate the man and bring him pleasure, yet they also leave him oily, weak, and chained to a life he hates. The lizard seems to represent lust and whispers all kinds of soul-destroying things into the man's mind.

In this story, an angel confronts the oily man and asks for permission to kill the lizard. The man, initially hopeful, asks if the lizard's death will hurt him, and the angel nods. This is undesirable; the man doesn't want the pain. He doesn't want the anguish of amputation, and he begins putting forward excuse after excuse. Sweat lines his face. The lizard makes its plea as well, bargaining for its future — in fact, screaming to be spared. But the angelic being comes back to the same question: "May I kill it?" "May I kill it?" Finally the man concedes — almost in a whisper — and the sword falls quickly on the lust lizard.

In a fantastic twist, the lizard doesn't die. It mutates. It begins growing into a living, energetic stallion. The horse stands strong and regal, and the man, formerly in bondage, is transformed as he mounts the back of the stallion and rides off toward a great light. Now strengthened, now fully alive, he travels to the place of joy, to the mountains where he may see the face of God. Lewis writes:

> Nothing, not even the best and noblest, can go on as it now is. Nothing, not even what is lowest and most bestial, will not be raised again if it submits to death.... Flesh and blood cannot come to the Mountains. Not because they are too rank, but because they are too weak. What is a Lizard compared to a stallion? Lust is a poor, weak, whimpering, whispering thing compared with that richness and energy of desire which will arise when lust has been killed.[39]

The real choice for the man was between pesky pleasures and imaginary comforts, genuine joy, and a rich, strong identity. That same choice is ours.

It is all about desire.

The happiest people who ever lived were not those with power and wealth — still less those who had sex with whomever they wanted. Those who experienced resounding joy were the ones who saw God in others and devoted themselves fully to the Jesus they saw there. Freudian thinking is quite mistaken: God is not a substitute for sex. The happiness of Hugh Hefner is pathetic and miserable compared to that of Mother Teresa or Desmond Tutu.

You and I have desires. We will never be rid of them. They are meant for our good and are only burdensome when we seek to fulfill them with things that cannot satisfy. Our desires can keep us pinned to shadows, or they can be redirected toward what is real. They can insist that we are mere animals, or they can awaken us to a new way of being human. The choice is ours. Will we desire the lasting or the transient? Freedom or bondage? Joy or Gehenna? The face of God or the illusions that lust offers? The decision is painful. It will require everything we are. But in the end there is only one choice that will make us happy.

6

WRATH AND THE MEEK PEACEMAKER

"Be angry, and do not sin."
PAUL OF TARSUS

In the mid-1990s, the funk rock band Rage Against the Machine took their lyrics seriously. Not only did they sing about fighting for the exploited; their lead singer, Zack de la Rocha, consistently left his rock star lifestyle to physically support an armed revolutionary group in one of the poorest states in Mexico.[1] He worked for farmers forced into severe poverty because of the practices of affluent businessmen. Many Rage Against the Machine lyrics rail against the abuses of capitalism and its fruit. One song, "Calm Like a Bomb," speaks of economics and perverted justice that leave "fields full of slaves" and dead children. What is de la Rocha's solution? Be "calm like a bomb. Ignite. Ignite. Ignite. Ignite. Ignite. Ignite. Ignite. Ignite. Ignite."[2]

The lyrics call listeners into battle against those who injure the helpless, whose greed would leave an entire culture destitute. The song emphasizes physical resistance and closes with de la Rocha, in a hushed voice, saying, "There's a right to obey and there's a right to kill." This is not a proverb; this is an assignment. Kill those who oppress the weak. When the poorest die because of someone's love of money, the oppressors ought to be vaporized. Ignite. Ignite. Ignite.

The band — longing for justice — turned to violence.

The film *Gandhi* — which won the Academy Award for Best Picture of 1982 — has a scene in which two lines of refugees move past one another — one Muslim, one Hindu. Both groups have been displaced. The government handed down divorce papers because neither group could live with the other, and India split off a chunk called Pakistan. This solution produced casualties. The scene begins with the tear-filled face of a man who is walking in one of the lines. We watch his dry, dirty face, marked by fresh tears, and then the camera pans downward. The man, moving through the desert, is holding a dead boy — his son. A victim of the forced exodus. The weeping man looks down again and again as he keeps walking. Then he looks to his left across a dry riverbed where a line migrates in the other direction. "My son is dead because of them," he thinks. "They killed the boy whose laughter once filled my life." His hands clench. His eyelids quiver. The man ignites. Running into the trench, he throws stones at the other line of refugees; profanities and rage flow from his soul. He is not the only angry person. Travelers from both lines suddenly pour into the riverbed with shovels and sticks. Both sides fight for the sake of their people. Both sides have been unfairly injured. Both sides — longing for justice — turn to violence.

A few months after September 11, I had a conversation with my brother about what we were doing on that day. Josh has the multi-platinum satellite TV package, and when he heard the news that morning, he began flipping through the stations until he landed on a feed out of Mexico. He didn't stop there for the commentary; he didn't stop because he's learning a new language. He stopped because this station didn't put any filters on its content. My brother watched human beings jump from flaming windows and fall and fall and fall. He saw their bodies explode when they hit the ground.

He saw graphic footage of limbs and blood covering the Manhattan pavement. As with so many, the pain he saw sat heavy on him. Upon reflection, he and I both affirmed that had the president used his address to the nation that night to say, "Hey, it's time to sign up and go kick someone's butt," we would have said, "Mr. President, I've got a nice pen and some real hard boots." In one afternoon, our longing for justice would have trumped our jobs, our families, our futures — and we would have turned to violence. We would have hit back as hard as we possibly could.

There is great pain in our world, and our anger alerts us to the fact that it needs fixing. We become angry when we see the weak exploited, those we care about injured, what we value destroyed. The desire for justice is legitimate. In fact, God desires the elimination of evil even more than we do. Yet when our longing for justice turns to violence and scorn, we no longer share God's perspective. We move from being part of the solution to becoming part of the problem. We move toward *wrath*, another face of sin at work in our world.

Dante called wrath a "love of justice perverted to revenge and spite."[3] The easy answer to injustice is fighting back. It takes no intellect or goodness of soul to start swinging at those who hurt us. In a good world that has been spoiled, violence, retaliation, and scorn are some of the spoiled parts. Once blows are thrown, words are spat, guns are pulled — or worse — all we create are more holes in God's good world.

When I was in high school, I loved the game Risk, and I would play it on the library computer with a few friends before school because, yes, I was that guy. Now, I wasn't very good, so one day I decided to take the program home and practice. I quickly found a way to win without much effort. I would get the other countries fighting one another, and once they had exhausted their resources, I would come in and wipe them out. It was easy to win, because if you can get people fighting each other, it is easy to destroy them.

This principle plays out in the book *Needful Things*, in which author Stephen King depicts the normal flow of life in a small Maine town.[4] As in any other town, bitterness, secret resentment, envy, and scorn bubble just beneath the surface, but the people trade only gossip and an occasional threat — until the devil moves in.

In the story, a new character opens a store and begins selling people fantastic items — things they have only dreamed of owning. A pair of Elvis's glasses, a sliver of wood from Noah's ark, an autographed baseball card needed to complete a prized collection. Yet the devil does not want money for these items. Instead, he asks his customers to do him simple favors — things he calls pranks. "You know Mrs. Jerzyck down the street? I want you to throw mud on the white sheets hanging in her yard." "You know the drunk who frequents the bar downtown? I want you to slash his tires." "You know the lady who bakes pies on the corner? I want you to skin her dog."

The victims of these pranks immediately assume that their rivals, neighbors, even their friends have done these awful things, and all the repressed issues suddenly come screaming to the surface. Within days, violence erupts everywhere across town as people march out to defend their precious dignity. As the book climaxes, the streets are filled with normal men and women out for justice with guns and sabers in hand, hacking one another to bits. The devil, of course, stands on the street corner, hat cocked, smiling — because when you get people fighting each other, it is easy to destroy them.

What happens when the world is shaken up a bit? What happens when poisons the world hasn't dealt with are stirred? Wrath plays on our inability to forgive, our inability to deal with injustice with intelligence. Wrath is nothing more than the act of hitting back.

Sometimes I actually think that if I can hit someone harder than they can hit me, maybe next time they won't swing in the first place. If I can hit someone harder than they hit me, I will feel better. If my blows connect, justice will be done. My fist, my tongue, my spit, my gun will set the world right.

This kind of lust for revenge leads to problems like those we see today in the Middle East, where even the young fight over and over again about past injuries — against adversaries who likewise are fighting over and over again about past injuries. They have not yet proven who can hit back hardest, and it seems the only things produced over time are more injuries. What makes retribution dangerous is that victims seldom stop thinking of themselves as victims and are unlikely to exercise self-control when the gun is finally in *their* hands. Wrath often escalates from small, if unknown, causes to the point where all shots are described as "return fire."

Hell, of course, laughs and swallows the bodies.

Ultimately, wrath is a deadly sin because it separates us from those we ought to embrace and cherish as fellow children of God. Wrath moves us away from those we could potentially spend eternity with. As is the case with lust, Jesus said that those who let wrath take hold in their hearts cast themselves into Gehenna; like lust, wrath throws our bodies and souls into that same pile of flaming trash:

> "You have heard that it was said to the ancient people, 'You shall not murder'; and anyone who commits murder shall be liable to judgment. But I say to you that everyone who is angry with his brother shall be liable to judgment; anyone who uses foul and abusive language will be liable to the lawcourt; and anyone who says, 'You fool,'[5] will be liable to the fires of Gehenna."[6]

Yes, wickedness hurts us. When the sins of others target our joy, our welfare, and those we love, we rightly long for things to be made right. *Wrath, however, is not concerned with restoration but with revenge and dominance.* Therefore, wrath aimed at our fellow human beings is always opposed to God's activities. Like the other deadly sins, wrath wars against the community — the kingdom — that God wants to create.

THEY WILL BE CALLED CHILDREN OF GOD

During the last week of Jesus' life, nearly everyone in Israel prepared for a war. Masses of pilgrims gathered in Jerusalem to celebrate the exodus and their ancestors' deliverance from slavery — all the while thinking of their own bondage, their own pain, their own reasons to pick up swords. The pilgrims sang emancipation songs as they approached the city of King David, every stanza affirming that the God who had split the sea and supplied manna in the wilderness would once again make them free.

The Roman occupation of Jesus' day had been particularly cruel. As a sign of humiliation and supremacy, the Romans had desecrated the Jewish temple with pagan images, oppressed the Jewish people with high taxes, and crucified all who opposed them. Though Rome allowed large gatherings such as the Passover, they watched the festivities closely for any sign of revolt.

The chief priests — stewards of the Jewish people — were responsible for the lives of tens of thousands of pilgrims entering Jerusalem that week. They were responsible for dealing with both Rome and their fiery countrymen and women. Far from being a burden, this responsibility had a reward. The religious elite enjoyed comfortable lifestyles and great power because of their talent for compromise. That year, however, they found it much more difficult than usual to keep pilgrims calm, for many believed the Messiah had come at last — the one who would retake David's throne and rule Israel again with justice and the blessing of God. Had this Messiah not been a man claiming to be the Son of God, perhaps the chief priests, too, would have followed him. But according to the religious leaders, anyone who listened to the man from Nazareth should have realized he was a heretic. The only remedy for such men was spelled out clearly by Moses: they ought to be executed with divine blessing.

Yet the masses endorsed Jesus. He drew large crowds wherever he went, and many claimed that he healed all the sick he touched. A rumor was even spreading concerning a man who had died in Bethany, just a short walk from Jerusalem. After lying in a tomb for four days, the man from Bethany was raised back to life by the would-be Messiah.[7] Though the religious elites concluded this was an obvious lie, it had spread quickly through the ranks of pilgrims coming to Jerusalem for the Passover.

The chief priests and their council had few solutions to the growing excitement. The drums of war were beginning to bang loudly. If Jesus decided to start a revolt, Rome would surely come and crush Jerusalem. The Romans would erect fields of crosses outside the city walls and nail the bodies of pilgrims and their families to them. The situation was explosive. The masses had gathered, longing to see God move on their behalf. The religious elite were alarmed and desperate. And hundreds of Roman soldiers were already in the city, prepared to do everything necessary to keep order and maintain their dominance.

As Jesus mounted a donkey outside of Jerusalem, he unleashed a perfect storm.

On Palm Sunday, two processions entered Jerusalem — one from the west, where Pontius Pilate and his entourage of military cavalry came into the city with swords, armor, and all the trappings of empire,[8] and another from the east, where Jesus rode into the royal city to the waving of palm branches, just as Judas Maccabeus had done two hundred years earlier when he kicked out the Syrians. It was a sign to all that Jesus had come to do business. Many pilgrims arriving for the Passover celebration surrounded Jesus as he moved toward the city, singing the psalms of festival time:

> When hard pressed, I cried to the LORD;
> > he brought me into a spacious place.
>
> The LORD is with me; he is my helper.
> > I look in triumph on my enemies.
>
> All the nations surrounded me,
> > but in the name of the LORD I cut them down.
> They surrounded me on every side,
> > but in the name of the LORD I cut them down.
>
> I was pushed back and about to fall,
> > but the LORD helped me.
> The LORD is my strength and my defense;
> > he has become my salvation.
>
> I will not die but live,
> > and will proclaim what the LORD has done.
>
> Open for me the gates of the righteous;
> > I will enter and give thanks to the LORD.
>
> I will give you thanks, for you answered me;
> > you have become my salvation.
> The stone the builders rejected
> > has become the cornerstone;

the LORD has done this,
and it is marvelous in our eyes.

Blessed is he who comes in the name of the LORD.
From the house of the LORD we bless you."[9]

This psalm — sung on the Mount of Olives as Jesus descended into Jerusalem[10] — begins with the language of conflict and ends with pilgrims making their way to the temple on Mount Zion to worship. This psalm (among many others that may have been sung) has heavy overtones of war and God's triumph over a tyrant.

Now, after decades of oppression, Jesus gave the people a reason to sing. Like a challenger entering the ring at the same time as the champion, Jesus' timing and body language told people he had come to deal with the enemies of God. Jesus was the one through whom God would exercise his wrath. Many of those singing had prayed for years that someone empowered by God would come and, like Joshua entering Canaan or Gideon fighting the Midianites, drive out the pagan occupiers and reclaim the former glory of Israel. Jesus possessed that power. Not only could he raise the dead and heal the blind; Jesus could walk on the sea and feed thousands from simple items such as a few pieces of bread and fish. He commanded the weather with his voice, and, more important still, Jesus was a man of God. John the Baptist — a prophet to be sure — had anointed Jesus, and it was rumored that a voice from heaven spoke over Jesus that day. The solution to years of misery was here at last. Surely at Passover — the celebration of the Jewish exodus from Egypt — the Messiah would call on God to destroy the pagans and reconstitute Israel as the light of the world.

With palm branches in hand and shouts of "Hosanna" (a word of praise for God's coming salvation) on their lips, the people were expressing their expectation. Each palm branch was a vote for rebellion; each shout of blessing was a call to pick up the sword.

Everyone who understood the situation began taking sides. The pressing questions that week were whether the thousands of festival-goers would follow this new Messiah into battle and whether the power of Jesus would be enough to overcome the brutal hand of Rome. In short, was God truly on Jesus' side? Would God act through this man from Galilee? Jesus entered the city of David riding a donkey, the symbol of Israel's new king.[11] If he was not the heir to the throne — if God failed to act through Jesus — then calamity was certain.

Then Jesus began to act in a radically unacceptable fashion. Instead of seeking the support of the religious elite, he condemned them with harsh language. Jesus stepped into their territory — the temple itself — and judged it a failure, calling it a mere pile of stones[12] and a hiding place for those who had robbed the Jewish people of their identity.[13] Jesus told the crowds derogatory stories about the religious leaders, calling them disobedient,[14] wicked shepherds of God's people,[15] men whose work — and even whose temple — was like a fruitless tree that deserved to be tossed away.[16]

Very early that week, the religious elite, defamed and humiliated, sought vengeance. In their wrath, they decided to kill Jesus. An opportunity dawned when one of Jesus' own followers — a former Zealot revolutionary now disenchanted with Jesus' methods — came to them looking to jump ships. Judas Iscariot heard in Jesus' message the language of certain defeat.[17] It seemed that the closer Jesus drew to Jerusalem, the more he talked about his own impending death.[18]

Yet the other disciples were willing to fight and to die if necessary. That week, Peter had said in front of everyone that he would go to prison — even give his life — for Jesus.[19] Peter had prepared himself to pick up the sword long ago when he guessed rightly that Jesus was the Messiah and had been told that hell itself would not stand against them as they neared the holy city.[20] The other disciples were also prepared for battle, collecting swords[21] and asking when they might use them.[22] As the week ended, everyone from the chief priests to the disciples, from the Roman legions to the mass of pilgrims, was willing to kill to see their god's kingdom come. To see justice done, they were each willing to ignite.

Jesus alone did not act according to this script.

The only death Jesus prepared for was his own. Jesus led his disciples to a garden on the east side of the city. There he wrestled with his impending execution for many hours. Though he had eluded arrest and murderous plots before, this time when armed guards came for him, Jesus surrendered willingly. The disciples had not expected this. They were sleeping when the armed men carrying torches, lanterns, and weapons entered the garden and awakened them.

Holding to his promise, Peter was the first to act. He began swinging the sword he had kept hidden. Certainly God would give him the strength and guidance he needed to slay the enemies of his king. Even if he were to die, he would die defending what was right, warring against evil, killing those who suppressed justice. And it was at this moment that he heard a voice: "Put your sword back in its place, ... for all who draw the sword will die by the sword. Do you think I cannot call on my Father, and he will at once put at my disposal more than twelve legions of angels?"[23]

Here Jesus categorically said that the way of wrath is not the way of God. We should take notice that when the opportunity came for one of Jesus' followers to use violence against the wicked, to establish justice through aggression, it was God himself who restrained Peter's hand.

Jesus knew that evil is overcome in a different way.

On Friday morning, when the Passover lambs were being prepared to be sacrificed later that day, Jesus stood in the dock at two trials.[24] After a quickly drawn-up midnight hearing, the temple authorities agreed to push for Jesus' execution. Unable to kill him themselves, the religious elite bound Jesus and took him to Pontius Pilate, the Roman governor of Judea. Pilate was Caesar's official representative. He could request all the power of the Roman Empire and get it. The chief priests came to Pilate claiming that Jesus was a revolutionary — a would-be Messiah, one who claimed David's throne: "He stirs up the people all over Judea by his teaching."[25] Hearing the accusations, Pilate turned to Jesus and asked, "Are you the king of the Jews?"[26] Pilate's sarcasm was thick. "Are *you* — a beaten, chained peasant — the king of the Jews?"

Yet this was the only charge the religious elite could muster. They argued Jesus' guilt as a rebel and said he was a direct threat to Caesar. Pilate thought the high priest and his entourage were jealous of Jesus' popularity.[27] Not wanting any part of this circus, Pilate decided Jesus' fate through the vote of those gathered outside his stronghold. Pilate paired Jesus with an insurgent murderer named Barabbas,[28] and those outside in the darkness chose the violent man instead of the one who promised peace.[29]

At this point the chief priests pressed on, demanding Jesus' execution. Pilate was still confused. In Jesus he saw someone he could destroy with ease. In order to emphasize the point and show the lunacy at hand, "Pilate took Jesus and had him flogged. The soldiers twisted together a crown of thorns and put it on his head. They clothed him in a purple robe and went up to him again and again, saying, 'Hail, king of the Jews!' And they slapped him in the face." Pilate then came out and addressed the Judeans: "Look, I am bringing him out to you to let you know that I find no basis for a charge against him." As Jesus was brought out, Pilate said, "Here is the man!"[30]

Instead of releasing the one he clearly saw as innocent, Pilate made Jesus a toy with which to mock the temple aristocrats. It's as though Pilate were saying, "If this man had any power at all, I could not do this. He is no threat to me. He is no threat to Rome, and if you had any sense, he would not be a threat to you either." Yet the religious elite pushed even more vigorously for Jesus' crucifixion.[31] At this point Pilate gave up. In a final act of mockery, Pilate said to them, "Here is your king,"[32] and Roman soldiers took the beaten man away to be crucified.

The soldiers marched Jesus through Jerusalem to a hill outside the city. They nailed a board to the top of his cross that displayed his name and his crime, and then they nailed Jesus there, lifting him high above the land so that all could see his broken body from the highways leading into the holy city. Here Jesus would die naked and friendless. When his dead body was brought down late on Friday evening, it seemed that all promise of a new kingdom had died with him.

Yet in God's grandest irony, Jesus' death was not a defeat; it was a royal coronation.

In the early hours of Good Friday, Jesus had confirmed to the Roman Empire that he was king.[33] A military escort then took Jesus out before the people. The crowd shouted for him and no other to take the throne.[34] Soldiers took Jesus away and draped a royal robe on his bleeding back. They crowned him and knelt before him, all singing, "Hail!"[35] The representative of the Roman Empire then presented Jesus, dressed in royalty, to the religious elite. "Here is the man!" Pilate said to the priests. "Here is your king."[36] The soldiers then paraded Jesus through town, with Jews and Gentiles alike lining the streets to see him.[37] Jesus then marched to the highest place in the land to sit on his throne — the saddle of a cross.[38] Priests, soldiers, and relatives surrounded him while a servant gave him wine,[39] and a sign overhead proclaimed, "THIS IS JESUS, THE KING OF THE JEWS," written in the three great languages of the day.[40]

On Good Friday, Jesus was enthroned for the entire world to see.[41]

As darkness covered the land, a lone point of light shone out. Looking at the dead body of Jesus, a pagan soldier knew that the sign above was not an accusation but a reality. He knew the crown was real, the robe had been real, and the cross he helped raise was truly a throne: "And when the centurion, who stood there in front of Jesus, saw how he died, he said, *'Surely this man was the Son of God!'* "[42] It was the title that emperors reserved for themselves. It was printed on their coins alongside *Pax Romana* — Roman peace.[43] As the centurion looked up at the body of Jesus, he saw one worthy of the greatest title in the land. To be called a son of God was the highest praise, for it meant that you were the true reflection of divinity.

Jesus' rejection of the way of wrath is clearly displayed in his death. Jesus did not use the enormous power he possessed to decimate the wicked. Instead, Jesus attacked the sin at work among his killers by suffering for them. Where Jesus' enemies placed him on the road to destruction, Jesus opened to them the way of life. The words of the centurion were apt, for as Jesus had taught earlier in his life, "Blessed are the peacemakers, for they will be called children of God."[44]

EVERYTHING IS GOD'S

Jesus told us what being a child of God looks like: "Very truly I tell you, the Son can do nothing by himself; he can do only what he sees his Father doing, because whatever the Father does the Son also does. For the Father loves the Son and shows him all he does."[45]

This picture would have been familiar to his listeners. Many fathers taught their sons as apprentices in their workshops. *Apprentice* means literally "side by side."[46] For Jesus, those who are children of God will be side by side with God, watching his hands, learning how he does things, discovering what he values, observing what he discards — and they will do what he does.

Jesus' most detailed picture of his Father is found in the parable of the prodigal son, and in this story Jesus depicts the father doing just two things — welcoming those who have hurt him and reconciling those who despise one another. The father in this story is a peacemaker.[47]

The prodigal son is a wonderfully layered story, and the interaction among the characters runs deep. In Jesus' tale, the younger brother insults his father and leaves, but it is the older brother, not the father, who refuses to forgive the younger son when he returns.

Often you and I get most angry not when someone has hurt us but when someone hurts those we care about. Yet if you and I are called on to be peacemakers, we usually have a relationship with one or both of the parties involved. If we are in a position to make peace, it means we will hurt along with one of the fighting parties. We will have to surrender our own rage. We must learn to forgive early. If you and I are to reflect God, we must care first for the unity of estranged brothers and sisters, despising what separates them. The peacemaker — one who would be a child of God — must dispose of wrath in order to reconcile the divided.

Notice further that in order to bring peace, the father in Jesus' story reminds his older son who he is: "My son, . . . you are always with me, and everything I have is yours."[48] I find this to be a beautiful phrase. The peacemaking father appeals to his son's identity. Jesus seems to be saying that in his Father's kingdom, the older brother doesn't need to fight for stuff. It's all his already.

Likewise, one of the reasons we may pursue peace with passion is that we don't have to squabble over rights or position or the past, for in God's eyes we lack nothing. In fact, you and I could live gentle, unassertive lives and still find that in God's kingdom we would not go without, for we presently possess all that is God's. We could be the meekest of the lot and still find that because we are the Father's daughters and sons, you and I will receive all that matters. Jesus said it this way: "Blessed are the meek, for they will inherit the earth."[49] Inheritance and sonship go hand in hand. Those adopted by God gain all that is his, and as we saw earlier, being a child of God is not following a list of to-dos; it is a call to change one's whole identity.[50]

Where peacemaking sounds proactive, even aggressive, meekness sounds spineless. The meek are those who get stepped on a lot, who are sweet tempered in response to the world's assaults. When I have heard people speak on this passage about the meek, they often say, "Meekness is like a strong stallion at rest. It is power under control." But this is a misunderstanding. Throwing a stallion into the first few beatitudes doesn't make sense. Again, the Beatitudes begin with an invitation — an invitation to spiritually poor, mourning, empty, and, yes, unstallionlike people. We might understand Jesus as saying, "Blessed are the considerate and tender, blessed are all you who are humane and harmless, because everything the conquering hordes have stolen, everything that the self-indulgent masses have squabbled over, will slip from their hands and be given to you."

What an incredible thing to hear! In Jesus' kingdom, the harmless and kind will gain what tyrants and the violent spent their entire lives seeking to possess. In this short sentence, Jesus judged and called worthless all the world's power plays. He mocked such pursuits with matter-of-fact candor and said that those marginalized and oppressed by the strong will inevitably possess all the plunder.

Of course, it sounded contradictory to say that the weakest members of society would inherit the world, but Jesus knew it to be true, for the world was his and his alone to give. The word *mine* can't really be said by us about anything in the universe.[51] Everything belongs to God. When we say "mine," it is an illusion. Often the thing we get angriest about is someone taking "our" stuff. They took my parking spot, my girlfriend, my idea. They sang my song. They cut me off in my lane. They stole my coat. They are wasting my time.

But *none* of it is ours — it's all God's.

This has unique implications when we look at wrath. Jesus knew that those who fight for their possessions will actually lose them, for those who act out of rage against their enemies will no longer look like children of God: "You have heard that it was said, 'Love your neighbor and hate your enemy.' But I tell you, love your enemies ..., *that you may be children of your Father in heaven.* He causes his sun to rise on the evil and the good.... Be perfect, therefore, as your heavenly Father is perfect."[52]

In order for us to reflect God, we must reject wrath. There is no other way. We must live with open hands. Nothing is actually ours. When that which is most important to us is taken from us, we must recall our identity. In God's beautifully flipped-over world, those who would hold tightly to their possessions, status, and even loved ones — to the point where they attack thieves and enemies, to the point where they ignite with wrath — will lose all they care about. They will prove to all that they are not children of God, that they are unworthy of an inheritance.

Yet those who live out their identity as peacemaking children — though the world is stolen from their gentle hands — will find that they have lost nothing. Everything still belongs to their Father. Though they are disdained as meek by those who do not know better, they are heirs of everything good. They may pursue peace, even giving their whole lives away, without fear of loss.

A THIRD WAY

In a popular book a few years ago, a famous Christian told his son how to confront a bully: zero in on the bully's mouth, and when you have it in your sights, hit him there as hard as you can.

In *Wild at Heart*, John Eldredge wrote of how he thought "turning the other cheek" would emasculate his seven-year-old son: "You cannot teach a boy to use his strength *by stripping him of it*. Jesus was able to retaliate, believe me. But he chose not to. And yet we suggest that a boy who is mocked, shamed before his fellows, stripped of all power and dignity should stay in that beaten place because Jesus wants him there?"[53]

Eldredge loves Jesus. He even believes that Jesus taught the pacifist route, but that only those who, like Jesus, already know their strength should hold it back when hit. Eldredge wrote, "You cannot turn a cheek you do not have."[54] Seven-year-olds don't know their strength yet. If Eldredge were to instruct his son to turn his cheek, he believed it would turn the boy into a "passive and fearful" man who would "grow up never knowing how to stand his ground."[55]

The logic here is key. Eldredge is arguing that when someone is confronted by bullies, there are *only* two possible responses: submissiveness or violence, aggression or passivity. Thus, when he first heard about the bully harming his child, Eldredge lifted his son's tearstained face and gave him the go-ahead to swing away. "At that moment," wrote Eldredge, "[my son's] soul was hanging in the balance. Then *the fire* came back into his eyes and the shame disappeared."[56]

We might say that at that moment, his son ignited.

Though I enjoy much of Eldredge's work, I think he is quite wrong here on two fronts: first, he thinks violence will strengthen his son, and second, he thinks turning the other cheek is about letting others abuse us.

Jesus was not a pacifist in the lie-down-and-let-others-run-over-you sense. Such passivity is more akin to sloth than any virtue. (If we must choose between wrath and sloth — hit or be hit — then it's little wonder we have difficulty with Jesus' turn-the-other-cheek teaching.) No, Jesus affirmed — and died displaying — a brilliant third way. It is the aggressive, dynamic targeting and elimination of the sin within his enemies. Simply turning one's cheek without reason is an apathetic move. But Jesus surrendered his body to his assailants in order to belligerently combat the soul-destroying sin within them. With each blow he received and each nail pounded into his flesh, he may have rightly said over and over, "This is my blood shed for you."[57]

Jesus' sacrifice of himself is a highly *proactive* move. He demonstrated a way of addressing his enemies that was neither passive nor violent, but restorative and God reflecting. He taught his followers to do likewise: "Do not resist an evil person. If anyone slaps you on the right cheek, turn to them the other cheek also. And if anyone wants to sue you and take your shirt, hand over your coat as well. If anyone forces you to go one mile, go with them two miles.... But I tell you, love your enemies."[58]

When the text says, "Do not resist an evil person," another way to translate it is, "Don't react violently against the one who is evil." The Greek word for "resist" is *anthistēmi* — a combination of the Greek *anti*, meaning "against," and *histēmi*, meaning "to cause to stand."[59]

Jesus is saying, in effect, "Don't knock over the person who is evil." Why not? Because there is a far better way to address evil and violence without contributing more evil and violence. Again, in a good world gone spoiled, retribution is part of the spoiled part. Jesus gave three examples of a better way to address injustice.[60]

First, when you are struck on the *right* cheek, Jesus said not to hit back but to offer your other cheek to an assailant, which invites a question. Why specify cheeks? Who cares which cheek? Jesus' contemporaries knew perfectly well. A slap to the right side of the face meant you had been backhanded. The backhand was reserved for inferiors. Masters used backhands against slaves, husbands against wives, Romans against Jews. The intention of the backhand was to humiliate, to put someone in their place — and in each case, if you were the one being beaten, physical retaliation would have been suicidal. Backhands were used when it was clear that the person being hit had no possible comeback.[61]

Why wouldn't such people have been slapped on their left cheek? Backhanding someone's left cheek would require an assailant to use his left hand, but in Jesus' culture the left hand was not used to interact with others. People took care of all their bodily nastiness with the left hand. No one used their left hand to interact with others. In fact, even to gesture with the left hand had serious consequences.[62] Handshakes, waves, even assaults were performed with the right hand.[63]

So what is the logic of turning the other cheek? Well, notice that if your *left* cheek is turned toward an assailant, he cannot use the back of his right hand. A backhand would break your nose, and that's not the point of a backhand. Again, the backhand was used to humiliate. The only way an assailant could use his right hand to strike your left cheek would be with his fist. If the assailant wants a clean hit, he will have to throw a punch. But here is the sheer brilliance of Jesus' teaching: *fists are only used in fights between equals.* Far from being a passive act, turning the other cheek says to an assailant, "Punch me and make me your equal, or else you are a coward." By turning the other cheek, the assaulted strip their oppressors of the power to dehumanize them. This is an overt act of nonviolent defiance, as well as a bold affirmation of one's self-worth.

In the next example — "If anyone wants to sue you and take your shirt, hand over your coat as well" — Jesus referred to the poorest of the poor, who would have had nothing but the clothes on their back. The "shirt" would have been a piece of inner clothing — essentially one's underwear — and the "coat," the outer clothing. We might ask, "Who would want to take the underwear from a poor person?" It's not like this is choice fashion or a valuable commodity. Again, the issue is humiliation. Only the poor have underwear and a robe as their only assets, and only the cruel want to take them.

To such people, Jesus said, "Don't just give them your underwear; give them all of your clothes." This seems a strange encouragement, but imagine such a scene in a court of law. Imagine the verdict comes down — "This man will now take your underwear" — and instead of disrobing in private, a poor man strips down to nothing, then holds out all his clothes to his oppressor. I generally try to avoid naked people in public places, and I imagine it would be awkward for someone to approach a naked man in court, let alone take the clothes from his hands.

Furthermore, it is dishonorable to look at those who are nude. Think of someone in our culture who is caught looking at pornography. Only the truly crass view such material in public. Likewise, in Jesus' culture indignity fell on the one who looked at or interacted with the naked. In offering up both underwear and an outer garment, those left with only humiliation suddenly seize the power, and the person suing them takes only worthless cloth and shame. Again, this was a nonviolent reaction to injustice that both affirmed the humanity of the oppressed and stripped the oppressor of his power to humiliate.

The last example may have been more common still. Roman soldiers in Jesus' day could make a peasant carry a load for up to one mile — but no farther.[64] So as to not exploit their oppressed subjects too harshly, the Roman army had severe penalties for soldiers who forced a peasant more than a mile. Jesus encouraged the exploited to go an extra mile for their oppressor because, as with the previous examples, by going a second mile the exploited take the initiative. The soldier is put in a position of chasing the peasant, asking, "Please, sir, give me my stuff back." Humiliation is shifted to the impotent soldier, and the oppressed again affirms his humanity and self-determination.

In all three examples, Jesus offered what Walter Wink calls "a third way." Not the way of violence, and not the way of pacifism. Jesus prescribed aggressive, nonviolent, rehumanizing retaliation. The three scriptural responses found in this passage shame those who rely on humiliation to get what they desire. More than this, these responses are all overt acts of love. Each moves not to destroy but to awaken — to tap the humanity within an opponent who has fallen under the power of sin.

This is not pacifist pomp. This is not wishful thinking or an impossible course. Any watering down of these prescriptions is a rejection of Jesus' own death. It was Jesus who when struck turned his other cheek,[65] who when asked for his shirt gave his coat as well,[66] who when forced to carry a heavy burden[67] went even farther for the benefit of his killers. Though it looked as though the powerful had humiliated him and left him to die, they were inadvertently pulling back the curtain of reality to reveal the world's true Lord and inviting him to rule.

In his revolutionary meekness, Jesus inherited everything. As a peacemaker he was truly worthy of the title "Son of God."

7

GLUTTONY AND THE PERSECUTED

My love is my gravity.[1]
AUGUSTINE OF HIPPO

A LARGE MOUNTAIN RISES ABOVE CARBONDALE, COLORADO. IT IS not the tallest mountain in the state, but because there are no other peaks around it, Mount Sopris looks enormous. It fills all the space to the south. You see nothing else.

I climbed the mountain with my family a few years back. It was a day hike up a long series of switchbacks. We moved above timberline toward the ascending ridge without much difficulty. Most of the climb was smooth, and some even jogged up the trail.

Nearing the thirteen-thousand-foot peak, I rounded a corner, looked back for my wife, and nearly stepped off the back side of the mountain. Without warning I had reached a small shelf of ground holding me over a sea of empty space. The cliff slid straight down for hundreds of yards toward a distant field of scree and boulders. The sight made me stop to balance, check my footing, and remind myself of death just a step away. As I looked over the edge, the weight of nothing-at-all filled my chest — and the nothingness had power.

Before Eve and Adam ate the forbidden fruit, it was as though they saw the cliff and then decided to jump from God's good world out into the nothingness.

Refusing to eat the fruit — which Adam and Eve may have done for many years[2] — had been the primary demonstration of their love for God. By declining the poisoned fruit, Adam and Eve affirmed daily that the world God had made was good, that they desired inclusion in the life God gave them, and that they cared for their Maker. Abstinence was a sign of faithfulness and commitment.

Conversely, eating the fruit was a rejection of God, his world, and a future married to him. More than anything else, consuming the fruit was an act of divorce. Like adulterers seeking another lover, Adam and Eve did not need the fruit hanging in the middle of the garden. It was excessive. They chose it for an extra measure of satisfaction.

Thus, the event in the garden was not about sex or violence. It was not even about pride, as some have argued.[3] Eating from the tree of the knowledge of good and evil was an act of *gluttony*. Adam and Eve took far more than they needed. They believed they could do whatever they wished with God's creation for their own pleasure and benefit. These gluttonous desires drew humanity into the nothingness, and it took their lives.

Notice how this deadly sin destroys us. Gluttony is not about obesity; gluttony is about what we unite ourselves to. Gluttons wed themselves to meals over and above what is good for them — and by devouring more and more, they have less and less.

The truth is, some who are physically overweight are not gluttons at all. They may have low metabolism or glandular problems or a job that requires them to spend all day sitting at a desk. More surprising still, an eighty-pound anorexic may be a raging glutton. Weight is not a sure indicator of this sin. The skinny suffer from gluttony as easily and as often as the stout, for gluttony is, first and foremost, excessive. It is a third car when one will do, a third drink when one is best, a third hobby when the other two you started aren't satisfying enough. Alcoholics and drug users are gluttons, but so are some Web surfers, card players, and businesspeople. In other words, "-aholic" is the suffix attached to the glutton's meal of choice, for gluttony is immoderation, and immoderation is not about having body fat; it's about having a gaunt soul.

In one sense, gluttony is about us — our bodies, our need for more experiences, more DVDs, more vacations, more clothing, more collectibles, more stuff. But like all expressions of sin, gluttony is primarily about separating ourselves from others. Gluttony is the temptation that most often succeeds in drawing us away from our duties. The deadly aspect of gluttony is always twofold. Immoderation not only emaciates our mind and heart; indirectly it lets someone else starve. Those who consume more than they need deny the excess to others, and in a world like ours, where human beings die from lack of food, water, and medicine, the gluttony of a culture or an individual can mean death for those who ache for our table scraps.[4]

Perhaps this is why gluttony has always been associated with food. In cultures where people on the street starved to death, the moral priorities of a fat man would be evident to all. He ate over and above what he needed when he could have given the excess to those he saw begging.[5]

That same spirit is alive today when someone purchases a new luxury automobile, builds an excessive closet to fill with excessive clothes, eats out consistently, or just plain spends money without any sense of frugality.

Imagine a person walking beside a lake in $500 shoes. He is enjoying his afternoon in the summer air, when looking to his left he sees a small girl who has slipped off the dock and is struggling to keep her head above water. Certainly it would be immoral of that person to think, "You know what, I would really like to save that little girl, but if I jump into the lake, I'll ruin my shoes." Surely if we heard of someone standing on a dock while a young girl drowned in calm waters close to shore, all because he thought more highly of his $500 shoes than the child's life, we would consider that person a monster. In fact, we would think him worthy of some punishment. *Yet what is the difference between this man saving his shoes and this man buying $500 shoes in the first place?* Surely he could have purchased similar shoes for fifty bucks, and the excess could have provided the medicine, nutrition, clothing, and schooling needed to help one desperately impoverished little girl not only survive but thrive in her poverty-stricken country. I have a hard time seeing a hole in that argument, and I think Jesus would agree.

Jesus didn't command the ascetic life, but he certainly didn't frown on it. He once said, "Where your treasure is, there your heart will be also."[6] Follow the money in Western culture, and we will find some of the shallowest and most worthless homes for our hearts. It has been noted in numerous studies that if just American Christians gave away the traditional 10 percent of their income (rather than the current average of 2.6 percent),[7] in a short amount of time the extra giving could nearly eliminate world hunger and unsanitary drinking water. The excessive lifestyle of just American Christians — very few of whom lack basic provisions — is indirectly starving the rest of our planet. The question, in light of our own gluttonous tendencies, is how much do you and I really need? What is a healthy basic lifestyle, and what is simply excessive?

When gluttony takes root in our hearts, it divorces us from the life that God has made good. It demands over and above what is natural. Immoderation is by definition a lack of balance. We see this in the story of Eden.

After Adam and his wife ate the forbidden fruit, the ground that gave them food became filled with thorns and thistles. Pain accompanied childbirth. The relationship between a wife and a husband fractured; instead of equality, one was inclined to dominate the other. Gluttony threw everything out of order. On the day the couple ate the fruit, the garden became a desert, the animals Adam had cared for became wild — and with the swords of angels, God mercifully removed his children from the garden so they would not live in that dead condition forever. And it was all because of dysfunctional appetites.

Sin entered the world through the *body* of a man and a woman. And it would take the body of another man to remove it.

In the Garden

In ancient times (and even today), rulers made images of themselves — normally statues or currency — and placed them in far-off cities so everyone would know what they looked like. Such rulers wanted their images implanted in their subjects' minds. They wanted people everywhere to understand who they were and what they were like.

We see this idea in Genesis 1. After God created the world, the last thing he made was a man in his own image. He placed him in the middle of his creation. Adam would reflect God's likeness for the whole world to see. The gospel writer Luke even called Adam "the son of God."[8] But God's image had cracked. Adam, Eve, and their children failed to fully reflect the God who made them, and a final consequence of their brokenness became apparent. All the ideas about God became confused. No one knew who God was anymore. Many years later, standing before Jesus himself, Pontius Pilate asked,

"What is truth?"[9] But Jesus was the new Adam, the last Adam neces-sary.[10] In his flesh, Jesus would show the world once again what God looks like.

Mark and Matthew both begin their stories with Jesus retreating into a desert.[11] At the beginning of creation, Adam had been given the task of guiding all the animals and naming them,[12] but Mark makes clear that in the desert around Jesus, the animals were wild. So too the ground was no longer a garden like Eden but a wilder-ness — a place without rule. When the Spirit led Jesus into the desert country, nothing in that world was ordered. The life of Eden was gone. And as Jesus walked through the land scorched by Adam's glut-tony, he began to fast.

Jesus picked up where Adam had failed. In the wilderness, Jesus was tempted by another serpent. As with Adam, the Devil poked at the good desires Jesus had, but he offered only toxic ways to meet them. The first temptation thrown at Jesus, like the one given to Eve, was an appeal to Jesus' appetite: "If you are the Son of God, tell these stones to become bread."[13] The Devil invited Jesus to put his physical needs above everything else.

The second temptation began the same way. The Devil took Jesus to the highest point of the temple and said, "If you are the Son of God, throw yourself down."[14] The crowds at Jesus' death repeated this same temptation as Jesus hung from the cross[15] — and for the same reason: the second temptation tried to entice Jesus to prove his identity, to prove he was God's image bearer. The temptation must have been appealing to Jesus. If he were to prove his identity through power, then perhaps he would not have to suffer. He could merely rule as he was made to.

But that is not what God looks like. By following such a temp-tation, Jesus would have failed to bear the very image that he was commissioned to show the world. And this is where the last of the three temptations hits: "Kneel to me, and I will give you the kingdoms of the world."[16] The Devil offered Jesus the goal of his life; he offered Christ the nations without persecution or death. As with Adam and Eve, the only cost to Jesus would be divorce from the Father.

Looking at each temptation, we notice that all of them were invitations to Jesus to destroy himself — through separating himself from God's call, jumping from buildings, and kneeling to evil. Like a nearby tree with forbidden fruit, these three temptations followed Jesus for the rest of his life on earth. They accompanied Jesus even to his last hour.

Yet by abstaining, Jesus did what Adam could not. He would be raised up so the world could see God again.

On the night before his death, Jesus entered a new garden to wrestle with the same temptations that had been Adam's downfall.[17] As with Adam, Jesus' thoughts were directed toward a tree. The question was not whether he would eat its fruit, but whether he would drink its cup. God's Spirit led Jesus to this garden not to escape the world but to restart it, to be a new kind of human. Like gluttony, this event would take place in and through Jesus' body. But instead of indulging self, Jesus would give himself for others.

It was an opposite and counteractive feat. In Jesus' flesh the holes in God's world would be mended. It would not be easy. In fact, Jesus prayed for God to take this cup from him. Yet the curse was firm. God told Adam and his descendants, "By the sweat of your brow you will eat your food until you return to the ground."[18] And as Jesus thought of the tree from which he would hang, he began to sweat. The thorns and thistles of the sin-infected earth would soon pierce his brow, and then his body would return to the ground. Like Adam,

Jesus would receive into his body death, evil, and all that separated humanity from what was good. But unlike Adam and his children in whose bodies sin lived, through Jesus' body sin and its fruit would die.

It was then that Judas led the chief priests and temple guards to the Mount of Olives. Those with swords led the Son of God from the garden — like Adam before him.[19] In the morning, Jesus was raised over the earth, and as God had worked for six days to create the world, so Jesus hung on the cross six hours to restart it. Nailed to the cross, forgiving his killers, suffering for his beloved, Jesus succeeded where Adam and all of his lineage had failed, for on the cross all the world was again able to see God.

With Jesus' limp body hanging still, a soldier took a lance and pierced the flesh next to Jesus' heart.[20] Jesus did not move, for he was dead. Adam, too, had fallen into a deep sleep in the garden, and God, in the stillness, had reached into his side and removed a rib. From that rib God fashioned for Adam a beautiful companion. And as the soldier's lance slid from between Jesus' ribs, "a sudden flow of blood and water" burst from Jesus' side. From that blood and water, Jesus would make for himself his own eternal bride.

In the ancient creation account, God made human beings on the sixth day — on Friday. A new Friday had passed, and as in days of old, God looked on that Friday, and he saw that it was good.

Fragrance

Every building associated with my wedding has been gutted or leveled. The church where we were married is now a day care. Our rehearsal dinner restaurant is now a drugstore. The city removed our reception hall and built an ice rink in its place. The university we attended bought my wife's home and made it a parking lot. My old apartment is now an architect's office. Everything about our world that day has been torn down and replaced with something else.

It's a telling picture of what happens in marriage.

When we marry, we enter a new life. Our old life was meaningful and valuable, but it gets taken apart and united with another life. The two truly do become one. My moods become her moods, my dreams become her dreams, my keys become her keys (and I hope to see them again someday). Marriage is a total union. When we unite with our beloved, we become something fundamentally different.

The Scriptures use marriage as a picture of our relationship to God. Jesus referred to himself as a bridegroom, and his ministry is likened to a wedding feast filled with new wine, where no one fasts.[21] One of the Bible's last images is of a wedding where the faithful have made themselves ready and are united to God forever in the age to come.[22]

The life of heaven is a marriage. When Jesus said that the kingdom of heaven is at hand, we should read this as "The wedding has commenced."[23] Empty humanity is being fundamentally reconnected with God. People from all over the world are now entering the chapel halls, and all four gospel writers tell a similar story to show what the wedding looks like.

Three days before his death, a young woman named Mary pulled out her only treasure and broke it at Jesus' feet.[24] The white jar filled with very expensive perfume had been her mother's.[25] It was the last thing she had to remember her by. It may have been her grandmother's, perhaps even her great-grandmother's. The jar was her ancestry, and she had hoped to give it to a daughter of her own. More than anything else, the jar was her future. It held the precious perfume, representing Mary's ability to fancy a husband. Without the jar, she would have to live with her brother for the rest of her years. Without it, she would become an object of mockery at gatherings. Her lack of a husband would ring loudly in her mind as she entered the synagogue or observed celebrations and holidays alone. Her sister and cousins might even discuss behind her back what a wasted life she had led.[26] Without the jar and its contents, no one would see her as beautiful. No one would desire her.

We might say that in the jar were Mary's identity, her status, and all her hopes of being united to a good man.

The house was full when Mary entered. Her brother, Lazarus, was reclining at the table with Jesus. The disciples sat with one another, excited about the festival and the impending revolution. Mary approached Jesus, and as she looked into his eyes, she broke the jar, pouring the precious perfume over his head. The party hushed as the room filled with the exquisite fragrance. Mary then let down her hair — shaming herself, her brother, and her family — and began wiping Jesus' feet with the oils. Everyone watched. No one approved. One man spoke for all, calling the act a waste.[27]

But Jesus silenced them. "Leave her alone. She has done a beautiful thing to me. She has prepared my body for burial."[28]

His words pierced the gathering — not because of the rebuke but because everyone believed Jesus would soon take the throne as the king of Israel. Wasn't that why they were going to Jerusalem? "To proclaim freedom for the prisoners" and "to set the oppressed free"?[29]

But Mary seemed to know what everyone else did not. This man who had done so much for her would soon die, and her knowledge made the gift even more profound. By breaking the jar, Mary wrote out her future as one consisting of a life of poverty, scorn, and loneliness. She chose to die for the sake of the soon-to-be-dead man before her. But the jar, which represented her future union with a good man, fulfilled its true purpose.

In dying to herself, Mary was united to Christ.[30]

The story of Mary is one of only a small set told in all four gospels not only because it contains one of Jesus' prime teachings — that in order to find your life, you must lose it — but because this is the anointing of Jesus Christ.

Christ means "anointed one," and it was in this act of total self-giving love that the anointing took place.[31] Mary's anointing of Jesus was not done by mere holy oils; the anointing of Jesus was done with an object that fully represented the whole life of one who loved Jesus. Contrary to the opinion of Judas and the other disciples, who saw only a rare perfume in a nice jar, what Mary broke at the feet of Jesus was her heart. Her whole life was poured out there before the sneering masses for the sake of her beloved. Yet the scent of her life given to Jesus filled the room with an exquisite fragrance.

The picture is one of union between Mary and her beloved. The picture is one of Jesus and his church. This picture is one of the life of heaven — humanity united to God.

When Jesus said, "Blessed are those who are persecuted because of righteousness, for theirs is the kingdom of heaven,"[32] this is the image he had in mind. Whereas the gluttonous unite themselves to what will ultimately kill them, the persecuted, having been united to Christ, give up even what they need for the sake of their beloved. Those who are persecuted are blessed with the kingdom — union with God — for they experience the hardship of a lover.

Eden was once union with God, but Adam and Eve sought divorce. Through the cross, Jesus restored Eden's beauty and initiated a new proposal to everyone, everywhere, to be wed once again.

FACE-TO-FACE

In his book *The Seven Habits of Highly Effective People,* Stephen Covey notes three habits of character and three habits in relationships that traditionally successful people employ. The seventh habit, the one that binds the other six together, he calls "sharpening the saw." All six habits, he says, will become dull if they are not consistently sharpened. So the seventh habit is crucial. It makes all the others thrive.[33]

In this same way, gluttony sharpens the saw of sin.

Pride longs for applause, but gluttony needs to be a diva. Envy covets what others have, but gluttony counts every insignificant detail. It is not enough to be slothful; gluttony abandons virtue in excess. Gluttony is salt when the greedy taste their spoils. One million dollars isn't enough; it must be ten million. Five-year-old wine isn't good enough; it must be fifteen years old — and French. Lust wants another woman; gluttony wants them all. Wrath wants revenge; gluttony wants the infliction of it to be creatively painful. At its most demonic, gluttony amplifies the other sins, enhancing their self-destructive power.

Jesus' blessing on those "persecuted because of righteousness" works in a similar and opposite fashion. When a light-filled life bumps into a dark world, the result is not moderate acceptance. Like the collision of cold air with a warm front, the result is a storm.

Some of those we think of as living highly virtuous lives were subject to severe forms of contempt. Mother Teresa was not praised by all her Calcutta neighbors for caring for those discarded in the gutters; she was insulted for affecting their karma. Martin Luther King Jr. was not admired by Southern gentlemen for seeking the reconciliation of all humanity as brothers and sisters; he was imprisoned and shot dead. And of course, Jesus was beaten and nailed to a pair of boards when he offered a better life to those in darkness.

Persecution is not a saw sharpener. Persecution shows whether our lives have been sharpened at all.

Thus Jesus said, "I have wonderful news for you who suffer because of your marriage to God: you'll experience heaven breaking into our world."[34] It is another outrageous paradox — another example of the world being flipped right side up. Notice that Jesus does not bless the overzealous or the obnoxious; he blesses those who, like committed lovers, suffer for their beloved's sake. This beatitude expresses the heart of heaven: sacrifice for the sake of another. Pictures of this kind of union with God color much of the New Testament. My favorite example is found in John's gospel.

Six months before his death, Jesus attended a festival in Jerusalem celebrating the Hebrew exodus, the time when the presence of God went with his people in the desert, providing water for them from the earth. On the last and greatest day of the festival, Jesus stood and said in a loud voice, "Let anyone who is thirsty come to me and drink."[35] No one came, but the words lit a storm. What Jesus said was not merely messianic.[36] These were words reserved for God alone.[37] Immediately the temple authorities came out and tried to put Jesus down. Over and over again, they told the crowd that Jesus had a devil, and they picked up stones to beat him to death. Yet Jesus slipped from the temple grounds and went out through the gates and into the street.

Outside the large temple walls sat a man who had been blind from birth, begging for daily bread from the festivalgoers. The disciples had spent many days celebrating God's provision, yet here was a man in need — just outside of God's temple, no less. Walking past the man, the disciples asked Jesus a question. They wanted to know why God allowed pain like this in our world. Why so much evil, Jesus? So they asked, "Rabbi, who sinned, this man or his parents, that he was born blind?"[38] Obviously, for them, if someone was in pain, then it had to be the victim's fault, right? "Tell us, Jesus. You're smart about these kinds of things."

And here, after this great feast where Jesus had revealed himself to the masses — where he was rejected by the religious authorities, misunderstood by festivalgoers, and so despised by some that they tried to stone him — here, when asked, "Why doesn't God do something about suffering?" Jesus knelt to the earth, as God had when he created Adam from the dust. He made some mud with dirt and spit and, with this application, healed the blind man. The miracle did not need to be unpacked. This was a highway sign reading, "I am the God I claim to be. I am the hope of humankind, and evil's days are numbered."

Amazingly, this is all set up. The author spends most of his time telling us what happened to this unnamed blind man once he began to see.

Jesus sent the man some distance away to wash the mud from his eyes. The man dunked his head under the water, and when he came up out of the water, he could see. Yet he could not see Jesus. Jesus had left. The man born blind only knew of Jesus and his gift through some kind of faith. But as the story proceeded, the man's faith began to increase. When he returned, his neighbors brought him before the religious law courts. When questioned, the unnamed man identified the one who healed him as "the man they call Jesus." Then he said, "He is a prophet." Finally, he said Jesus was "from God."[39]

Yet the more this man's esteem for Jesus grew, the more his troubles increased. First he was questioned by the temple authorities. Then he was left to fend for himself by his parents. Then he was kicked out of the temple and excommunicated, which meant that the religious faithful could no longer associate with him. The unnamed man lost everything because he stood for Jesus before those in darkness.

When Jesus heard that they had thrown the man out of the temple, Jesus found him and asked, "Do you believe in the Son of Man?"

After all these trials, the man asked, "Who is he, sir? Tell me so that I may believe in him."

The man had been persecuted severely because of Jesus, someone he'd never seen, and when he used the word "believe" — *pisteuō* in the Greek — he meant, "Tell me, sir, so I may *unite* with him. Tell me so I may *lay down all that I am* for his sake. Tell me so I may *commit* to him." These are the words of a man willing to give everything for a lover. And in response Jesus said, "You have now seen him; in fact, he is the one speaking with you." You have chosen to be wed; now here is your beautiful bride. To this the man said, "Lord, I *pisteuō*" — I commit, I entrust, I unite — and he worshiped him. As with Mary's pouring the perfume on Jesus' feet, these are wedding vows.[40]

The picture painted here is again of Jesus and his church — a church that was once in darkness, a church taken under the waters of baptism to receive new sight, a church that suffers for its Lover and has at times had all its worldly goods taken from it, a church often ostracized and even abandoned by those who once cared for it, but a church that nonetheless walks in faith, even though it has never seen its Beloved. And in the end, what happens?

Unity. The unity of Jesus and his church.

The question of gluttony and the persecuted is a question of marriage. What am I united to? What will I give everything for? The glutton's answer comes through addictive behaviors. Though we may say our first love is for God or for a set of human beings, our actions tell the real story. The glutton sells her soul for another hit, another car, another round of trivial pleasures, a forbidden fruit. The persecuted, on the other hand, gives even what she needs for the sake of her lover.

In 1 Corinthians 13, Paul ends his brilliant painting of love with this:

> For now we see only a reflection as in a mirror; then we shall see face to face. Now I know in part; then I shall know fully, even as I am fully known.
>
> And now these three remain: faith, hope and love. But the greatest of these is love.[41]

The love Paul described is the love shared between Jesus and his church.

We live in the time of trials, where we may be and often are forsaken by those we care about. We may lose friends and what we need for the sake of Jesus, but we also hear a distantly familiar voice: *Do you believe? Do you commit? Do you unite?* And soon, like the blind who see the face of their beloved for the first time, we will enter life where we are united with God forever.

8

THE STORY
GOD LOVES

If the doors of perception were cleansed,
every thing would appear to man as it is, infinite.
WILLIAM BLAKE

MTV AIRED A POPULAR SHOW A FEW YEARS BACK IN WHICH YOUNG people driving Swiss cheese with a steering wheel would call up the network for help. Nothing in these cars seemed to work. Stuffing was falling out of the front seats, rust had eaten away the floor, the air-conditioning didn't work, and a window or two wouldn't roll down. The show, called "Pimp My Ride," always began with a surprise appearance at the door as the host, Xzibit, would ring their bell. Invariably, the hapless car owner would lose it. They knew that when Xzibit arrived, they would soon experience something awesome: the car they had loved down to nothing was going to be remade. In fact, Xzibit and his friends would make it better than new; they would transform it into a wondrous piece of speed and sound and highway fury.

Naturally, the show was interesting for car guys who like blow-torches and subwoofer installations, but it gained an even broader audience because there is something awe-inspiring about watching an artist take that which is dead and make it alive again.

TLC has a handful of shows with the same theme. TLC is "The

Learning Channel," but it ought to be called "The Knock-Down-a-Bunch-of-Walls-and-Build-a-Ridiculous-Master-Suite Channel." Most of the shows on TLC are about upgrading houses. My favorites are the ones in which someone buys a crack house in Anywhere, California, installs stainless steel appliances, then sells the home for eight hundred grand. In these shows, entrepreneurs take something ugly and love it to the point where their souls ache. Often, repairing holes in these homes is not about waving a wand. Renovation is about sledgehammers. It's about bleach cleaner. It's about large Dumpsters filled with trash. But renovation is also about restoring cabinetry to its former beauty. It's about rejuvenating the mosaic tile work from the 1920s. It's about taking something that has foul places in it and transforming those places into something beautiful. These shows have gained a large audience for TLC because there is something awe-inspiring about watching an artist take that which is dead and make it alive again.

Nearly all reality television shows — at least the good ones — focus on restoration. Whether it's a home being renovated, a wardrobe being purged of spandex, or even one's body getting a makeover, we love to watch the neglected shaped artistically into something beautiful. We love the idea that nothing is beyond repair, the thought that what is rank can be transformed.

And we love this idea because God loves this idea.

Such stories appeal not just to our minds but also to our hearts, because we know in our bones that so much of ourselves and of our world is tragically out of joint and in desperate need of renewal. It will take someone with skill and time and, above all, love to patiently mold what is disgusting and fragile in us and make it teeming with fresh life again.

This theme appears over and over again in the Scriptures. God has not abandoned our world. Nor does he have a vacuum ready to suck out all the people he likes so he can destroy the rest. God has put his hands to work here. The material before him is often foul and nasty, but *the renovation is now.* And there is something awe-inspiring about watching a master artist take that which is dead and make it alive again.

Nearly every story in the Bible depicts something destined for the grave that suddenly experiences new life. From the elderly having children to imprisoned foreigners rising up to run an empire, from a nation of slaves finding freedom to barren women finally conceiving — all these stories point to something crucial in the character and passions of our Creator: God loves to raise the dead. This ought to give us hope, for the human story begins with a suicide.

The first few chapters of the Bible are a macabre procession of tales about death. The first humans eat from a poisoned tree, one of their children kills the other, nearly all the world is drowned. Looking at the lives of the earliest humans, the writer repeats the same phrase again and again:

"And then he died."

"And then he died."

"And then he died."[1]

It wasn't always like this. God created a good world filled with his kind of life, his kind of joy, fruit born from his rule and pleasure. He created human beings without insecurities or shame, and they walked in the refreshment of their Maker's presence. But that world is seemingly gone. You and I have inherited this infected one. Our world is filled with dysfunction. Wars are waged. Those we love die. Our flesh deteriorates over time. People and nations go mad, and tragedies mark the years.

More tragic still, we feel that same brokenness within us. And it's not just our flesh that's wasting away. Our souls are infected, and we all feel it.[2] We all know that something inside us is tragically out of sync. We cannot consistently be the kind of people we wish to be. I have failed so many times in some areas of my life that it often seems pointless to try to change. Even worse, sin makes the destruction of my heart feel so good, and I am truly torn. I hate yet cherish my addictions. I hate yet cherish my ability to control others with mean words. I hate yet cherish my excesses even as I see so many going without. I hate yet cherish the pornographic. I hate yet cherish the need to be the center of attention everywhere I go. I hate yet cherish tidbits of gossip and the destruction of people I don't like. I hate yet cherish all these poisons that jerk me to the ground, distort my freedom, and eat away my soul. In a relatively short time, I will die — and I wonder how much it all will have meant anyway. Won't I look back with just a mixture of regret and pain? My only hope is that God is not willing to leave those he loves in such a condition.

And this is the rumor being spread.

Remember what Jesus said in the parable of the sower: God has begun to scatter his seed, and the seed is beginning to sprout. Even in you and me, the roots are starting to expand. Buds are popping open, and in some places, fruit is even visible and ready for the tasting. It seems this world, so long neglected, is actually showing signs that point to a different kind of future — one without grief, one without sin, one even without death.

You and I live at a unique time. We may actually experience tastes of God's future in small bites, both in our world and within ourselves, and each taste signals good news about what God is presently doing. Each bite affirms that the God who made this world and made it good is creating new life in spaces that were once barren. It is a sign, like green shoots bursting up in early spring from the cold, hard earth. The fruit we experience speaks to us of our future, of how things should be, of how things will be.

That future has not yet come in full. God's elimination of sin is only now arriving. The fruit around us is more like an announcement of God's future. It is, in fact, an invitation to experience, to enjoy, and to desire more deeply the resurrected world ahead.

Doorways

After Moses rescued the Hebrew people from slavery in Egypt, they crossed into a desert. For forty years the early Hebrews traveled through the land between their enslaved past and their hope-filled future. As the people approached their new home, God had them send ten spies into a new land, a land far from slavery — the Promised Land. The spies brought back a report of what they had seen there, but their report was mixed.[3] Some of the spies feared the future and began spreading rumors that the Promised Land was devoid of life, a place where the inhabitants devoured all who came near. Yet others said, "No, it is a beautiful land, and, as God promised, it is filled with life. And though it may be difficult to gain, we ought to follow the God who freed us from slavery."

Two reports were presented to the people. Two conflicting accounts of the future. Two different ways of understanding reality. Whom should they trust? The audience would have experienced conflicting emotions — doubts and hopes, fears and faith. Nothing was certain. The evidence from the two sets of spies was all opinion mixed with bravado.

But one bit of information remained.

The spies had also brought something back from the land. They came carrying a pole on which was fastened a branch teeming with a large cluster of grapes. As these refugees listened to the reports of the spies, they fed on the grapes of the Promised Land.[4] In the midst of their decision to press forward, the Hebrews enjoyed the fruit of the future God had planned for them. It was an experience in the present of the life to come.

Though the assembly of Israelites stood in a wilderness — a place devoid of life, where only God's daily provisions kept them alive — they were tasting the reality of a new world. The fruit, of course, could not lie. It was simply a sign. Yet the grapes served as a dramatic appeal to the desire of the Hebrews to go forward, to leave the desert, to abandon any idea of returning to slavery, and to commit everything they were — their hopes, ambitions, treasure, and hearts — to the future God had for them.

Despite this sign, despite the taste of God's future, most of the people began to grumble. The road would be too difficult, the enemies too large. Many wanted to return to Egypt — to slavery — where things were familiar.

As it was with the Hebrews then, so it is with us today.

God has done all the work necessary to rescue you and me from slavery to sin, and now we stand in the space between our past and God's future. We live in the desert between the hell we long to leave behind and the heavenly reality we pray consumes every cell of our bodies. It is the shadowlands. Hell is still with us, and heaven is all too slowly breaking in. Saved from a world of darkness, we still must peer through the gray of a world in which the full light of day has not yet dawned.

Unfortunately, we have the same minds, the same tendencies, as our Hebrew forebearers. We live our lives knowing both the happiness and the hardship of slavery. We know that often it is just easier to obey forces that would keep us chained to a life we hate. We know that if we return, many of our longings will be met, but we also know that our old life is weak and disheartening. It is a life of soul-ache. It is a life from which — in our better moments — we once cried out for rescue.[5]

Like our forebearers, we live in a world of doubt. We do not know exactly where we are going. We're unfamiliar with the scent of the air ahead. We have not seen the God we pray to. We have only promises and hopes. Sometimes these hopes feel clear and alive, but often they are misty, faint, and seemingly so distant. We look at those we journey with, and sometimes we see conflict and confusion. Sometimes our leaders and heroes fail, and it all seems like just a noble lie. The farther we go, the more we realize that moving forward often means death — death to more of myself, my agenda, my preferences, my interests — for the sake of others. *And none of it seems to have a guarantee attached.* Here we are, sitting in a desert between two lives — one of slavery and one of death and uncertainty.

Yet in our desert, God meets us with fruit from his future, fruit of a renewed and restored world.[6]

When the will of God is done here and now, the result is heaven breaking into our lives like clusters of large grapes carted around in the wilderness. We enjoy now the eternal kind of life Jesus wants us to enjoy forever. When we eat together, laugh together, sing together, and serve together, we experience the flavors of heaven. When we feed the hungry, clothe the naked, heal the sick, house the homeless, and die to ourselves for the sake of another, we enjoy the heavenly feast. When we listen to the Scriptures, participate in Communion, love our enemies, and cancel debts, heaven breaks into our desert world. More than anything, when we hear the voice of God telling us that we are loved, that our many sins are forgiven, that we are his children, we experience now what we will experience forever.

The story of the grapes comes from a book in the Old Testament called Numbers. Numbers got its name from two lists — one that begins the book, another that ends it. One is a catalog of the names of those who began the forty-year journey through the desert; the other was composed on the banks of the Jordan, listing the names of those who crossed into the Promised Land.[7] These two lists have a single glaring quality. The first is filled with the names of the dead; the latter is a book of life.[8] The first list is composed of the people who wanted to return to slavery, who did not desire more of the fruit God had offered them. The other list is of people entering a new world of hope who are presently leaving the desert and entering God's future. The former is a list of rebellion and disintegration; the latter is one of faith and persistence. Those whose names were recorded at the beginning of Numbers ultimately died in the desert; those named at the end entered God's Promised Land.

One detail set apart those made alive from those who died: their response to the grapes God offered in the desert. Did these people desire the fruit of God's new world? This alone determined which book contained their names, *because fruit is a doorway*. When the serpent held out fruit in the garden of Eden, those who ate it entered death and brokenness. When God held out fruit in the desert, those who ate it and believed entered his Promised Land. And on the night before he died, Jesus took wine — a drink made from the grapes of Israel — and he said, "Drink from it, all of you. This is my blood ..., which is poured out for many for the forgiveness of sins."[9] The drink was freedom. The drink was the doorway to God's renewed world.

The Torah ends with a sermon (recorded in Deuteronomy) spoken at the same time that the last list was taken in Numbers. In the sermon, Moses said to all who would enter God's future, "This day I call the heavens and the earth as witnesses against you that I have set before you life and death, blessings and curses. Now choose life, so that you and your children may live and that you may love the LORD your God, listen to his voice, and hold fast to him. For the LORD is your life."[10]

Moses invited the people to choose the reality God orchestrates over the void that sin leaves scratched into our world. That same choice is ours. In our own desert, with signs of God's future all around us, we choose whether to move forward or to remain in our own wasteland.

BEHOLD

When Jesus began to preach his Sermon on the Mount, he was offering fruit to refugees out in the wilderness.[11] The Beatitudes were the taste of grapes for those stuck in the desert. In these Beatitudes, Jesus showed his followers a picture of heaven. He painted God's renewed world and reminded them that, though they were beaten down and miserable, God was on their side and wished them nothing less than absolute joy.

So too with us. In the Beatitudes, we see who is truly fortunate. Though the desert around us seems tedious, difficult, and harrowing, and though it is a long haul that has even taken the lives of those we love, we must affirm daily in confession and prayer that the alternative — remaining chained to the seven deadly sins — is suicidal. Happiness does not come with chains. As we saw in the parable of the sower, happiness is a desert wilderness suddenly transformed and overflowing with the reality of God's rule, with the fruit of his future.

And we taste the fruit from God's new world when the poor in spirit fill God's kingdom. We taste the fruit of God's new world when comfort comes to those who mourn, when the meek inherit the earth, when God's fullness enlivens those who hunger and thirst for a right soul. We taste the fruit of God's new world when mercy is poured out on the merciful, when the pure in heart see God, when the peacemakers are known universally as God's sons and daughters. We taste the fruit of God's new world when the persecuted take their places alongside the prophets with gladness, knowing that their suffering is not vanity but is union with Christ. Among so many other details of God's future, the Beatitudes are heaven breaking into our desert world and filling it with the life of God's future.

When we dedicate ourselves to this vision — to a world turned right side up again — we partner with God in the restoration of this world. It was a divine, holy calling for the spies to bring the fruit of God's future back from the Promised Land to people in the desert. It is no small chore to convince those in the wilderness that God's reality is in fact the ultimate reality — that the way of sin is simply a cancer eating away at us, at what we were made to think, enjoy, and become.

The Beatitudes, made real in our lives, are signs to everyone of where humanity and our world are headed, for the world itself is moving forward toward a new day when evil will be eliminated, sin will be overwhelmed, and all of creation will burst with the fruit God bears in and through humanity. God's reign will cover everything; the trenches dug by sin will be filled in, and all things will be whole again. At the very end of the Bible, God says, "There will be no more death or sadness. There will be no more crying or pain. Things are no longer the way they used to be.... I am making everything new!"[12]

Jesus began his Sermon on the Mount with the Beatitudes and his portrait of God's coming kingdom. He ended the sermon by declaring that those committed to his vision are "like a wise man who built his house on the rock. The rain came down, the streams rose, and the winds blew and beat against that house; yet it did not fall, because it had its foundation on the rock."[13] Those who make Christ's perspective their own will stand strong forever. God created a good world where living souls could thrive — where the life connected to creation, to other creatures, and to the Creator is heavenly.

Conversely, Jesus showed in his teachings and parables that those who serve pride will be left alone.[14] Those who serve the fires of lust and wrath will burn up in their flames.[15] Those who serve envy and sloth will experience a dark exile.[16] Those who serve greed will lose their very lives.[17] And those who serve gluttony will starve for the only life there is.[18] In each case, the fruit of sin is spoken of by Jesus as fire and darkness, death and solitude. Those committed to the nothingness to the nothingness will go. As C. S. Lewis wrote, "I notice that Our Lord, while stressing the terror of hell with unsparing severity, usually emphasizes the idea not of duration but of *finality*. . . . [Hell] is in no sense *parallel* to heaven: it is 'the darkness outside,' the outer rim where being fades away into nonentity."[19]

The seven deadly sins are the best description of life in hell. The real question for all of us is not whether we will someday go to hell but whether we will ever come out. The seven deadly sins are both the invitation into hell's fires and the temptation to stay, to prop a pillow behind our heads, and to kick the holes all around us bigger.

Our world is charged with both the grandeur of God and the void of his absence. All that exist are the heavenly reality and the hellish infection eating it away. It all comes together here. The deadly sins offer us meager fruit that decimates our world, our souls, and our hearts. Such fruit may look pleasing to our eyes and good for gaining what we desire, but it is poisonous through and through. Conversely, the Beatitudes are fruit from God's future. They are pictures of God's reign breaking into our world and enlivening it again, showcasing for all to see what a world empty of evil and filled to the edges with God's life will look like.

The deadly sins and the Beatitudes are two realities, each vying for our affection. The Beatitudes reveal the tenor of heaven; the deadly sins are the methods of hell. Both call us to serve them, to eat, to enjoy, and to believe. But only one draws us into reality. Only one promotes life.

And only one will make us happy.

NOTES, RESOURCES, DISCUSSION

INTRODUCTION: HOLES IN A GOOD WORLD

1. Ringside, "Tired of Being Sorry" (April 2005).

2. Quoted in Frederick Copleston, *A History of Philosophy*, vol. 2 (Garden City, N.Y.: Image Books, 1962), 84.

3. See Matthew 8:1–4; Mark 1:40–45; Luke 5:12–16. This is the second individual miracle described in Mark — and the first in Matthew. Mark has Jesus casting out an evil spirit from a man, then healing the sick — specifically this leper. Jesus' work is summed up symbolically by these two miracles. He overcomes the power of evil and then restores infected humanity.

4. Luke 8:1; see also Matthew 4:23; 9:35.

5. Mark 1:15.

6. Luke 8:5–8.

7. So says N. T. Wright (*The Resurrection of the Son of God* [Minneapolis: Fortress, 2003], 449). Notice the significant placement of this story in the Gospels. The story of the sower is one of seven parables told in Matthew, Mark, and Luke. There are five large teachings in Matthew, and this parable begins the third. Thus, this teaching is the very center of Matthew's account. Furthermore, the parable of the sower is the first parable told in Mark, which we may note was the first gospel written. Lastly, this parable precedes and is the lens through which we can understand the four miracles in Luke 8 — calming a violent storm, removing a legion of evil spirits from a demoniac, healing a sick woman, and

raising a girl from the dead. It is worth studying how the parable of the sower informs each of these miracles. Luke certainly sets it in such a place as to give them their meaning and purpose.

8. Mark 4:13 NLT. The NASB, KJV, and NRSV agree with the NLT's rendering.

9. Luke 8:8.

10. This is affirmed by the later interpretation Jesus gives in Luke 8:11–15.

11. What Jesus says here may have some bearing on discussions about the problem of evil. In fact, this may be the best expression of Jesus' theodicy.

12. Luke 8:8. Matthew 13:8 says the crop was "a hundred, sixty or thirty times what was sown." Mark 4:8 says, "some multiplying thirty, some sixty, some a hundred times."

13. See Matthew 21:33–46; Mark 12:1–12; Luke 20:9–19.

14. See Matthew 20:1–16.

15. See Luke 13:6–9.

16. Luke 8:10–15.

17. See John 1:1, 14.

18. E. P. Sanders, *The Historical Figure of Jesus* (New York: Viking, 1994), 11.

19. Matthew 6:10.

20. *Oh, God! You Devil*, directed by Paul Bogart (Warner Bros. Pictures, 1984).

21. See Matthew 10:39; 16:25; Mark 8:35; Luke 9:24; 17:33.

22. See Matthew 13:44.

23. Matthew 4:17; see also the parallel in Mark 1:15.

24. See N. T. Wright, *The Challenge of Jesus* (Downers Grove, Ill.: Inter-Varsity, 1999), 43–44. In fact, Wright hits on this idea in nearly every book he has written about Jesus.

25. This is a controversial point, but I think it makes the best historic sense. If you read the Sermon on the Mount, it does not sound like a sermon,

for sermons have a different kind of pacing. *The Sermon on the Mount, instead, sounds like a campaign speech.* It is pithy, to the point, and listy. You could replace "no lusting, no malice, no divorce" with "no tax cuts, no child left behind, no corporate greed." In my view, since Jesus was going from town to town, I think it makes sense to think of him communicating a similar message over and over — just like a stump speech — to his various audiences. If Jesus was calling Israel to come and be part of God's inbreaking kingdom, his first communication with them would need to be invitational and brief. It would need to lay out who he was and his view of what was most important for his early audience to hear — and the Sermon on the Mount does exactly that. Therefore, I reject theories that this sermon was given just once, was a compilation of many different teachings, or was created by Matthew and Luke for their purposes.

26. Luke also records four of these eight beatitudes (6:20–23). In this book, I will be focusing on the longer version found in Matthew.

27. See Matthew 5:3–6.

28. In this way, the teaching known as the Beatitudes functions very much like a later passage: "Come to me, all you who are weary and burdened, and I will give you rest. Take my yoke upon you and learn from me, for I am gentle and humble in heart, and you will find rest for your souls. For my yoke is easy and my burden is light" (Matthew 11:28–30).

29. See Matthew 5:7–10.

1

Pride and the Poor in Spirit

1. I've seen this story told in a variety of places. It is attributed to Ann Landers in "Heaven and Hell: The Real Difference," in A 2nd *Helping of Chicken Soup for the Soul,* ed. Jack Canfield and Mark Victor Hansen (Deerfield Beach, Fla.: HCI, 1995), 55. This reference ought to boost my scholarly credentials.

2. John Milton, *Paradise Lost,* book 1, line 263 (1667).

3. Quoted in Mark Water, ed., *The New Encyclopedia of Christian Quotations* (Grand Rapids: Baker, 2001), 828.

4. Author unknown; quoted in *The New Encyclopedia of Christian Quotations*, 824.

5. To draw them out of their pride. However, both James 4:6 and 1 Peter 5:5 remind us that God opposes all works of the proud.

6. See Stanley J. Grenz, *Theology for the Community of God* (Grand Rapids: Eerdmans, 2000), 187–88. In this beautiful work, Grenz wrote, "As we erroneously view ourselves as either better than or less than others, [this] leads to broken relationships" (p. 188). "Sin is marked by the disruption of the community that God desires for us and consequently for all creation.... [It] disrupts and seeks to destroy the community God intends to establish. Summarily stated, *sin is the destruction of community*" (p. 187; emphasis mine).

7. See Luke 15:11–32.

8. Of course, the dogs also reveal the extreme squalor and poverty of Lazarus.

9. In Greek lore, Hades is the realm of the dead. In the Old Testament, a similar place is called "Sheol," a word often translated "the grave." The belief in Jesus' day was that when you died, you did not go "up there" or "down there." Everyone went into the land of the dead, perhaps to await a resurrection from the dead. Revelation 20:13–14 later revealed that Hades/Sheol will be thrown into "the lake of fire" — which invites all kinds of interesting new questions about the nature of hell.

10. Luke 16:22–31.

11. In fact, when we look to this passage for insight into the afterlife, we miss the point. N. T. Wright affirms that this passage ought to be treated "as a parable and not as a literal description." See N. T. Wright, *The Resurrection of the Son of God* (Minneapolis: Fortress, 2003), 437–38; see also N. T. Wright, *Jesus and the Victory of God* (Minneapolis: Augsburg Fortress, 1997), 255–56, in which Wright provides a comprehensive list of other scholars who affirm this view.

12. Rob Bell shared this insight in "Jesus Wants to Save Christians: Part 7" (sermon, Mars Hill Bible Church, Grandville, Mich., November 5, 2006). See also Francis E. Gigot, "The Bosom of Abraham," in *Catholic Encyclopedia*, vol. 1 (New York: Robert Appleton Company, 1907); see http://www.newadvent.org/cathen/01055a.htm.

13. We see this in John 13:23, 25: "One of them, the disciple whom Jesus loved, was reclining next to him.... Leaning back against Jesus, he asked him, 'Lord, who is it?'"

14. Seether, "Fine Again" (2005).

15. "Treehouse of Horror X," episode 230, season 11, *The Simpsons* (October 31, 1999).

16. Many thanks to my friend Dan Self for this insight.

17. The phrase "and God saw that it was good" is repeated six times in Genesis 1 (see vv. 4, 10, 12, 18, 21, 25).

18. Genesis 2:18.

19. Genesis 2:18. It is, by the way, a beautiful thing to note that the word "helper" (TNIV, "[our, my, their] help") is also used to refer to God (Psalm 33:20; 70:5; 115:9–11).

20. Genesis 2:24.

21. Genesis 1:31 (emphasis mine).

22. Genesis 3:8.

23. One fascinating note here: God is walking in a Spirit-charged atmosphere *after* the man and woman eat from the tree. It's as though the entrance of sin into the world has not changed the fact that God's creation is bathed with the presence of his Spirit.

24. Matthew 6:9–10.

25. See Matthew 22:1–14.

26. See Matthew 18:21–35.

27. See Luke 15:11–32.

28. See John 3:16; 5:36; 6:38; 17:3.

29. See John 6:48–58; 10:11–18; 15:13; 1 John 3:16.

30. See John 14:26.

31. See Matthew 22:37–40.

32. Matthew 5:3.

33. Matthew 5:3 MSG.

34. Dallas Willard, *The Divine Conspiracy* (New York: HarperCollins, 1998), 100.

35. Robyn Griffith-Jones, *The Four Witnesses: The Rebel, the Rabbi, the Chronicler, and the Mystic — Why the Gospels Present Strikingly Different Versions of Jesus* (New York: HarperSanFrancisco, 2000), 115.

36. Richard J. Foster, Dallas Willard, Walter Brueggemann, Eugene H. Peterson, eds., *The Renovaré Spiritual Formation Bible* (New York: HarperSanFrancisco, 2005), 1800.

37. God doesn't want anyone to become or remain "poor in spirit." He desires us to be like Jesus, who is thriving with the presence and joy of all that God gave him. In fact, the opposite of the first beatitude is also true: "Blessed is Jesus Christ — one rich in spirit — for his is the kingdom of heaven." The first beatitude is not a prescription to *become* poor in spirit, to empty ourselves of spirit. (You ought to hold on to as much of the spirit God gives as you can.) But so too, God does not want us to deceive ourselves. If our tank is empty, the worst possible reaction would be to ignore it and drive into the desert.

38. Though the concept of human beings having *rûaḥ* is found all through the Old Testament, the word used in Genesis 2:7 for "breath" is *nᵉšāmâ*, which is the word depicting the physical act of breathing out of one's mouth. When God *nᵉšāmâ*-ed into Adam, the latter was indwelt by *rûaḥ*.

39. See Plato's *Apology*.

40. Some sins *are* worse than others, and in Jesus' mind, this kind of pride took the prime spot. Lust and greed separate us from God and others, but pride severs our relationships with fantastic efficiency. As a result, Jesus often spoke to sexual deviants and tax collectors with sympathy, but not to the proud. In fact, those who pretend — who hold forth in bold colors their religiosity yet fester within — received Jesus' harshest rebukes. "Woe to you, teachers of the law and Pharisees, you hypocrites! You are like whitewashed tombs, which look beautiful on the outside but on the inside are full of the bones of the dead and everything unclean" (Matthew 23:27). In fact, many believe that Matthew 23 is the contrasting sermon to the Beatitudes. Whereas the Beatitudes speak of the blessing of enjoying God's reign, all seven "woes" focus on pride. The seven woes are God's perspective on those who reject his life and fall into misery. At one point, Jesus even calls the teachers of the law

and Pharisees children of hell (Matthew 23:15), as though their true
father was the nothingness.

41. Of course, not all pain and struggle are remedies to pride, but it may be
that some are.

42. Thomas Aquinas, *Summa Theologica* II-II, question 162, article 6, reply
to objection 3 (emphasis mine).

2

Envy and the Mourner

1. See 1 Samuel 8:6, 19.

2. 1 Samuel 8:7.

3. See 1 Kings 11–12.

4. See Genesis 3 (see the beginning of chapter 7, where I comment on this
more).

5. See Genesis 4.

6. Genesis 27–28.

7. See Isaiah 14:12–15.

8. Socrates (469–399 BC), in Stobaeus, *Greek Anthology* III.38.48.

9. See Matthew 20:1–16.

10. Matthew 20:4.

11. If you are one who's doing the grumbling in one of Jesus' stories, you
are not in a good spot, for grumbling is the activity of those who left
Egypt — who, in the desert, desired to return to slavery and, as a result
of their grumbling, died in the wilderness.

12. Matthew 20:12.

13. Matthew 20:13–15.

14. See a similar use in Matthew 22:12.

15. See Luke 15, especially the setup for the three parables in verses 1–2.

16. See Matthew 20:20–28.

17. Matthew 20:22.

18. Psalm 23:1.

19. Consider Luke's version of the Beatitudes (Luke 6:20–22), which is followed by four "woes" (Luke 6:24–26).

20. Matthew 20:25–28.

21. Rob Bell, *Sex God* (Grand Rapids: Zondervan, 2007), 106.

22. John 20:25.

23. John 20:26.

24. James 5:16.

25. See Genesis 3:11. And yes, I do think that confession at this point would have been most helpful.

26. See Genesis 33. Notice how the language and events are the opposite of the prodigal son story.

27. Matthew 3:2; 4:17.

28. As a celebratory side note, I did get the teaching job six months later, but in that six months — of not having to worry about teaching seventy college students every other day — I began work on a series for Atlas called "Seven" and had a little extra time to work one of the messages into a chapter and a book proposal. So I'm fairly thankful for supposed blessings suddenly taken away and replaced with real ones that don't necessarily look like blessings.

29. Matthew 5:4.

30. Oscar Wilde, *De Profundis* (1905; repr., Mineola, N.Y.: Dover, 1997), 38.

3

SLOTH AND THOSE WHO HUNGER
FOR A LIFE MADE RIGHT

1. Peter Kreeft (*Back to Virtue* [Fort Collins, Colo.: Ignatius, 1992], 155) writes, "The person who never relaxes is not a saint but a fidget."

2. Blaise Pascal, *Pensées* (New York: Penguin, 1995), 131.

3. See Kreeft, *Back to Virtue*, 153.

4. Matthew 6:23.

5. Dante, *The Divine Comedy: Purgatorio* (New York: Oxford Univ. Press, 1939), canto 17.91–139.

6. See Matthew 25:14–30.

7. Matthew 25:21, 23. See also the parallel in Luke 19:11–27.

8. Matthew 25:25.

9. Matthew 25:30. Of course, Jesus thought being thrown from the master's home was not a step toward freedom but a move away from happiness.

10. Matthew 25:26.

11. Just before the parable of the talents, Jesus told a story about ten virgins who wanted to impress a man who was looking to marry (Matthew 25:1–13). Only a few of the virgins, Jesus said, prepared themselves for the man's arrival. The others were unprepared. So too, Jesus was saying that most of the culture was unprepared for God's return. They were like virgins who were desirous of a groom but who did nothing to win his heart. The parable of the talents specified what preparing for God's return meant. Readiness meant discharging all the duties the master left them with. Readiness is active, not passive.

12. See Matthew 22:1–14.

13. Matthew 22:13.

14. See Matthew 25:31–46.

15. Matthew 25:34, 41.

16. Matthew 25:40, 45. In this vein, George Bernard Shaw (*The Devil's Disciple* [Whitefish, Mont.: Kessinger, 2004], 30) wrote, "The worst sin toward our fellow creatures is not to hate them, but to be indifferent to them: that's the essence of inhumanity."

17. Genesis 11:4.

18. See Genesis 1:28.

19. See Genesis 3:8.

20. See Exodus 13:21–22.

21. See Exodus 40:34–38.

22. See 1 Kings 8:10–12.

23. See Daniel 3:22–25.

24. See John 1:14 among other Scriptures.

25. See chapter 8 for more.

26. Habakkuk 2:13–14 (emphasis mine).

27. See specifically the three parables in Matthew 25.

28. Acts 2:1–8, 11 (emphasis mine).

29. Acts 1:8.

30. See Revelation 21–22. Again, see chapter 8 of this book.

31. Matthew 5:6.

32. See Luke 15:11–32.

4

Greed and the Mercy Giver

1. Cited in Anup Shah, "Arms Trade — a Major Cause of Suffering," *http://www.globalissues.org/Geopolitics/ArmsTrade/Spending.asp.* See "World Wide Military Expenditures, *http://www.globalsecurity.org/ military/world/spending.htm,* for current spending trends, which in 2004 passed the $1 trillion mark. Of course, the United States accounts for roughly half of that.

2. See Carol Bellamy, "The State of the World's Children 1998: Focus on Nutrition, *http://www.unicef.org/sowc98/.* The figure of six million has particular weight, given that this was the same number of Jews killed in the Holocaust. Unfortunately, malnutrition was just one of the preventable causes of death for so many children. Many more died because of lack of cheap medicines and protection against malaria.

3. Thomas Hobbes (*Leviathan* [1651; repr., Whitefish, Mont.: Kessinger, 2005], 52) noted (rightly, I think) that man's chief fear is that of a violent death at the hands of other men.

4. Ecclesiastes 1:3, 14.

5. See Augustine, *The City of God* (AD 413; repr., New York: Modern Library, 1950). The city of man is a prominent theme throughout the work, particularly in the second half.

6. We often associate greed with money, and gluttony with food, but this is a mistake. Accumulation can be nonmonetary. Greed can assume more and more wives, homes, cars, clothes, tools, collectibles, experiences, or power. So too the glutton may cast aside moderation not only with food

but also with sex, alcohol, golf, cards, work, drugs, books, information, or television. These two sins ought to be divorced from their traditional association with just money and food, for their poison spreads much further.

7. Charles Dickens, *A Christmas Carol* (1843; repr., Whitefish, Mont.: Kessinger, 2004), 11.

8. *Wall Street*, directed by Oliver Stone (Amercent Films, 1987). Michael Douglas plays the role of Gordon Gekko.

9. Dante, *The Divine Comedy: Purgatorio* (New York: Oxford Univ. Press, 1939), cantos XIX, XX.

10. Ibid., canto XIX:121, 122.

11. Isaiah 44:18.

12. See James 4:1–2.

13. 1 Timothy 6:10.

14. See Matthew 26:6–16; Mark 14:1–10; Luke 22:1–6; John 12:1–6.

15. Matthew 6:25–26. Verses 19–21 say, "Do not store up for yourselves treasures on earth.... But store up for yourselves treasures in heaven.... For where your treasure is, there your heart will be also."

16. See Luke 6:24.

17. Luke 12:1.

18. Luke 12:15 (emphasis mine).

19. For more, see C. S. Lewis, *Mere Christianity* (1943; repr., New York: Macmillan, 1981), 137–41, 147–55, 159–64. Thanks to Rob Bell, from whom I first heard the distinction between *bios* and *zōē* applied to this passage ("Jesus Wants to Save Christians: Part 4" [sermon, Mars Hill Bible Church, Grandville, Mich., October 8, 2006]).

20. Luke 12:16–21.

21. Notice again the subtle incorporation of a garden.

22. See Edith Lederer, "UN: Hunger Kills 18,000 Kids Each Day," *Washington Post*, February 17, 2007, *http://www.washingtonpost.com/wp-dyn/content/article/2007/02/17/AR2007021700219.html*.

23. UNICEF, "The Progress of Nations 2000: The Power of Immunization," *http://www.unicef.org/pon00/immu1.htm*.

24. An outstanding resource that will help challenge this trend (without the guilt) is the World Vision weekly podcast, "World Vision Report," hosted by Peggy Wehmeyer, *http://media.worldvision.org/rss/wvus_podcast.xml*.

25. See Diane Brady and Christopher Palmeri, "The Pet Economy," *Business Week*, August 6, 2007, *http://www.businessweek.com/magazine/content/07_32/b4045001.htm*. The article went one step further in illustrating the lucrative spending on household pets. One scientist, it said, developed plastic testicles to replace neutered ones (because who wants a dog that doesn't look symmetrical?) at a cost of $919 a pair. As of August 2007, he had sold 240,000 pairs!

26. See Jeffrey D. Sachs, "Beware False Tradeoffs," *Foreign Affairs*, January 23, 2007, *http://www.foreignaffairs.org/special/global_health/sachs*.

27. Of course, we also need governments around the globe, but especially in the West, to commit their considerable assets to alleviating poverty — the most pressing problem in our world today.

28. See Jeremiah 1:10: "See, today I appoint you over nations and kingdoms to uproot and tear down, to destroy and overthrow, to build and to plant."

29. An insight shared by Rob Bell in "Jesus Wants to Save Christians: Part 4."

30. This isn't a specific saying of Jesus. The conclusion follows if you accept my interpretation of the parable of the rich fool.

31. Matthew 16:26.

32. Luke 10:25 and 18:18 (paralleled in Matthew 19:16 and Mark 10:17).

33. Luke 18:22.

34. Jesus told the opposite story in the short parable of a man walking through another man's field. As the man traveled, he saw the corner of a box. Opening the lid, he discovered a large treasure within. He did not snatch up the treasure like a thief. Instead, he went and sold all he had in order to purchase the field. He rid himself of everything, yet he acquired the valuable property — and so much more. (See Matthew 13:44–45.)

35. Luke 18:24.

36. See Luke 10:25–37.

37. Luke 10:30–35.

38. Samaritans adhered to a different understanding of Torah from those in mainstream Judaism in Jesus' day and worshiped at a different temple. More than this, many in Jesus' day viewed the Samaritans as having intermarried with pagan tribes, and so both in belief and in heritage the Samaritans had become a separate people from the Jews.

39. Luke 10:37.

40. Consider not only the parable of the rich fool (Luke 12:16–21) but also the parables of the unmerciful servant (Matthew 18:23–35), the faithful and wise servant (Luke 12:42–48), the sheep and the goats (Matthew 25:31–46), and the talents, or bags of gold (Matthew 25:14–30).

41. Irenaeus, Clement of Alexandria, and Origen all held this view (see, e.g., Origen, "Homily 34.3," in *Patrologia Graeca*, 13:1886–88. See also Linda McKinnish Bridges, "History of Interpretation," *http:// www.newmediabible.org/1goodsam/travel/07luke103637/articles/article 7histofinterpretation.htm.*

42. See Philippians 3:1–11.

43. "Saul [Paul] was still breathing out murderous threats against the Lord's disciples" (Acts 9:1).

44. John 20:22.

45. Dietrich Bonhoeffer — a devout German Lutheran — said, "The only man who has the right to say that he is justified by grace alone is the man who has left all to follow Christ." He concludes this way: "Those who try to use grace as a dispensation from following Christ are simply deceiving themselves" (*The Cost of Discipleship* [New York: Macmillan, 1963], 55). Only those who have begun to release the toxins in their lungs may take in the fresh breath of God's mercy.

46. See Romans 12:1–2.

47. Mark 8:35.

48. See Viktor Frankl, *Man's Search for Meaning* (New York: Simon & Schuster, 1984), 88–91.

49. See Matthew 21:33–46; Mark 12:1–12; Luke 20:9–19.

50. Mark 12:9.

51. Luke 12:48.

52. Acts 20:35.

53. Matthew 10:8.

5

LUST AND THE PURE OF HEART

1. I borrowed this example from C. S. Lewis, *Mere Christianity* (1943; repr., New York: Macmillan, 1981), 82–83.

2. Quoted in *The Lenten Triodion*, trans. Mother Mary and Bishop Kallistos Ware (South Canaan, Penn.: St. Tikhon's Seminary Press, 2001), Thursday of the fifth week of Great Lent, song 2, troparion 6.

3. Thomas Aquinas, *Summa Theologica*, II-II, question 35, article 4, reply to objection 2.

4. See Matthew 21:31.

5. See Peter Kreeft, *Back to Virtue* (Fort Collins, Colo.: Ignatius, 1992), 166.

6. Matthew 5:27–30.

7. See 2 Kings 16:10–18; 21:4–9.

8. The TNIV translates this phrase "Valley of Slaughter."

9. Jeremiah 7:29–33 MSG (see also Jeremiah 19; 32; 2 Kings 23; 2 Chronicles 28; 33).

10. Ezekiel 10 tells us that God's glory — his protective, guiding presence — left the temple soon after the reign of Manasseh, leaving the Hebrews vulnerable to the empires that surrounded them. See also Acts 7:43.

11. At this point in history, Israel had already split into a northern kingdom called Israel and a southern kingdom called Judah. The Assyrians had decimated the northern kingdom some years earlier (722 BC).

12. Gehenna is derived from the Hebrew *gai-ben-hinnom*, which means "Valley of the Son of Hinnom." In some rabbinical texts this is shortened to *gai-hinnom*, which is just a short jump to the Greek *Gehenna*.

13. N. T. Wright (*Matthew for Everyone: Part One* [Louisville: Westminster, 2004], 46) simply leaves the word untranslated — as *Gehenna*, not hell: "If your right eye trips you up, tear it out and throw it away. Yes: it's better for you to have one part of your body destroyed than for the whole body to be thrown into *Gehenna*. And if your right hand trips you up, cut it off and throw it away. Yes: it's better for you to have one part of your body destroyed than for your whole body to go into *Gehenna*." For Wright, it was essential to have his readers understand that Jesus is using a picture from his day here.

14. Though some have noted that even blind persons and those without hands can still be controlled by lust. It certainly isn't a cure-all.

15. C. S. Lewis (*Reflections on the Psalms* [New York: Harcourt, Brace & World, 1958], 41) wrote, "The moment 'Heaven' ceases to mean union with God and 'Hell' separation from Him, the belief in either is a mischievous superstition."

16. See Matthew 8:12; 22:13; 25:30.

17. See Matthew 10:28.

18. See John 3:16; 10:28.

19. The common view of hell is that it is the place where one is entirely separated from God. *Yet God is the ground of all reality.* It strikes me as incoherent to think those in hell continue to exist *and* have successfully separated themselves from the God in whom "all things hold together" (Colossians 1:17). Dear friends, the two are mutually exclusive. This invites more thought from all of us, myself included.

20. C. S. Lewis, *The Great Divorce* (New York: Macmillan, 1946), 65.

21. John 6:55.

22. Matthew 26:26.

23. Psalm 34:8.

24. Numbers 6:24–26.

25. Job 19:25–27 (emphasis mine). Notice the reference to resurrection in this passage.

26. Job strikes me as a soul-making theodicy. It's as though God says, "Look at all I have made. Isn't it obvious that I am making you as well, Job?"

27. See Revelation 22:4.

28. Psalm 27:4.

29. See, e.g., 1 Corinthians 6:19.

30. Examples are 1 Corinthians 3:16 and 2 Corinthians 6:16.

31. In other passages, Jesus says that what is done for the "least of these" is done for him (Matthew 25:40). Those like Mother Teresa who have lived out this passage have found it to be true. When they pick up abandoned children from the gutters, when they serve the lepers and the dying, they encounter Jesus.

32. Matthew 5:28 (emphasis mine). Jesus uses the infinitive verb form of *epithymeō* here (translated as an adverb ["lustfully"] in the TNIV). It is the only time it is used that way in the New Testament. See *The Strongest NIV Exhaustive Concordance* (Grand Rapids: Zondervan, 1990), 1551 (GK numbers 2121, 2123); see also *Vine's Complete Expository Dictionary of Old and New Testament Words* (Nashville: Nelson, 1985), New Testament section, 161–62, 384–85.

33. Luke 22:15. Note the strong wording, literally, "with desire I have desired."

34. 1 Timothy 3:1.

35. Philippians 1:23.

36. Both of these philosophies see the body as base or even evil. They posit that the real reason we are unhappy is because of this physical stuff in which we reside, and to be happy is to escape to the mental or the spiritual. It represents a dualistic way of thinking.

37. C. S. Lewis, *The Weight of Glory* (1949; repr., Grand Rapids: Eerdmans, 1965), 1–2.

38. Lewis, *Great Divorce*, 99–107.

39. Ibid., 106.

6

Wrath and the Meek Peacemaker

1. For more about this band, visit *www.ratm.com*.

2. Rage Against the Machine, "Calm Like a Bomb" (1999).

3. Dante, *The Divine Comedy: Purgatorio* (New York: Oxford Univ. Press, 1939), cantos XV–XVII.

4. Stephen King, *Needful Things: The Last Castle Rock Story* (New York: Viking, 1991). This, incidentally, is the single best book about the seven deadly sins.

5. The word Jesus uses for "fool" — *moros* — means "morally worthless." It is an attack on a person's heart and character. See *Vine's Complete Expository Dictionary of Old and New Testament Words* (Nashville: Nelson, 1985), New Testament section, 246.

6. Matthew 5:22 (as translated by N. T. Wright, *Matthew for Everyone: Part One* [Louisville: Westminster, 2004], 42). I use this rendering because most translations do not translate "Raca" — the term used by Jesus and translated by Wright as "foul and abusive language." For the sake of our discussion, leaving "Raca" untranslated can be confusing. Also, Wright does not use the word "Sanhedrin" — lawcourt — which in this context could also be confusing, given what I will say about the Sanhedrin later in this chapter.

7. See John 11:1–44.

8. See Marcus J. Borg and John Dominic Crossan, *The Last Week* (New York: HarperSanFrancisco, 2006), 2–5.

9. Portions of Psalm 118 — specifically, verses 5, 7, 10–11, 13–14, 17, 19, 21–23, 26. Observe the multiple references to the temple in verses 19–27. N. T. Wright (*Jesus and the Victory of God* [Minneapolis: Fortress, 1996], 498) notes that this song was "clearly designed to be sung by pilgrims going to the temple."

10. See Matthew 21:9; Mark 11:9; Luke 19:38.

11. See Genesis 49:8–12; 1 Kings 1:32–35; Zechariah 9:9.

12. See Matthew 24:1–2; Mark 13:1–2; Luke 21:5–6.

13. See Mark 11:11–18; 12:1–11; and parallels.

14. See Matthew 21:28–32.

15. See Matthew 21:33–46; Mark 12:1–12; Luke 20:9–19.

16. The movement of Mark 11:12–23 is certainly one of judgment on the temple itself. The temple on Mount Zion is like a fig tree without fruit, and it ought to be traded for something else (see Mark 12:9–11).

17. See Matthew 24:1–14; Mark 13:1–13; Luke 21:5–19. The final turn of Judas's heart came on Tuesday night when a woman with an expensive bottle of oil came to bless Jesus. After the woman poured the contents on his head, Jesus said to his disciples that she had anointed him for his burial. This would not be a comforting message to hear if, like Judas, you thought the kingdom of heaven would come through the military victory of God's Messiah. If Jesus expected to die, then he must not have thought he could win the battle against Rome and retake Israel's throne. Judas, who desired just such a victory, left the company of the disciples immediately and went to the chief priests. They would know what to do about a shepherd leading the sheep astray.

18. See, for example, Matthew 16:21.

19. See Matthew 26:35; Mark 14:31; Luke 22:33; John 13:37.

20. See Matthew 16:13–20.

21. See Luke 22:38. Jesus' emphatic "That is enough" has a double meaning. On one hand, he seems to be saying, "Those swords will do." But he is really saying, "I am tired of you not understanding me." Of course, he means the latter, for not long after this, he stops Peter from swinging his sword (see Luke 22:51).

22. See Luke 22:49.

23. Matthew 26:52–53. The number twelve here is significant, for it represents Israel. There were twelve tribes of Israel, and certainly the Father could have put them all at Jesus' command at Passover time, fulfilling the military messianic expectation.

24. One trial occurred before the Sanhedrin, the noblest and most developed religious order in history. The second was before the Roman procurator, a representative of the greatest legal system of the ancient world. Together these were the high points of humanity's ancient achievements, and together they failed. Jesus also stood before King

Herod (Luke 23:6–11), but this was far less like a trial than an exhibit at a circus.

25. Luke 23:5.

26. John 18:33.

27. See Matthew 27:18; Mark 15:10.

28. See Mark 15:7.

29. See Matthew 27:15–18; Mark 15:6–8; Luke 23:13–19; John 18:39–40. "Barabbas" means "son of the father." When Pilate offered the people a Son of God to have as their own, they chose the man with blood on his hands.

30. See John 19:1–5. "Judean" is often a far better translation of the word *Jew* in John's gospel. The word denotes a regional identification, not a religious one.

31. See Matthew 27:22–23; Mark 15:12–14; Luke 23:20–22; John 19:6–7.

32. John 19:14.

33. In John's gospel we read, " 'You are a king, then!' said Pilate. Jesus answered, 'You say that I am a king. In fact, the reason I was born and came into the world is to testify to the truth. Everyone on the side of truth listens to me' " (John 18:37).

34. See Matthew 27:15–23; Mark 15:6–14; Luke 23:18–22; John 18:39–19:7; 19:15.

35. See Matthew 27:27–30; Mark 15:16–19; John 19:2–3. We may note that Luke has Herod, "the king of the Jews," robing Jesus (Luke 23:11).

36. John 19:5, 14.

37. See Matthew 27:31–34; Mark 15:20–23; Luke 23:26–33; John 19:16b–17.

38. Crosses were often outfitted with a small seat-like notch where the body of a crucified person might rest. This was not done out of mercy. The saddle prolonged the execution (and therefore the agony) by allowing the crucified one to breathe more easily.

39. See Matthew 27:34, 41; Mark 15:23; John 19:25.

40. See Matthew 27:37; John 19:19–20.

41. Note Psalm 2. Here are a few excerpts: "The kings of the earth rise up and the rulers band together against the LORD and against his anointed [the Christ], saying, 'Let us break their chains and throw off their shackles.' The One enthroned in heaven laughs; the Lord scoffs at them. He rebukes them in his anger …, saying, "I have installed my king on Zion, my holy mountain.' I will proclaim the LORD's decree: He said to me, 'You are my son; today I have become your father. Ask me, and I will make the nations your inheritance, the ends of the earth your possession….' Blessed are all who take refuge in him" (vv.2–8, 12). I will return later to this theme of inheritance and the possession of the earth.

42. Mark 15:39 (emphasis mine).

43. See John Dominic Crossan, *In Search of Paul* (New York: Harper-SanFrancisco, 2004), 91, 98. The son of a god might be proclaimed as *divi filius* — son of the divine one.

44. Matthew 5:9.

45. John 5:19–20.

46. See N. T. Wright, *John for Everyone* (Louisville: Westminster, 2004), 62.

47. See Luke 15:11–32.

48. Luke 15:31.

49. Matthew 5:5.

50. See comments on the parable of the prodigal son in chapter 1, pages 35–36.

51. See C. S. Lewis, *The Screwtape Letters* (1942; repr., New York: Harper-Collins, 2001), 113–15.

52. Matthew 5:43–45, 48 (emphasis mine).

53. John Eldredge, *Wild at Heart: Discovering the Secret of a Man's Soul* (Nashville: Nelson, 2001), 78–79.

54. Ibid., 79.

55. Ibid.

56. Ibid. (emphasis mine).

57. See Luke 22:20.

58. Matthew 5:39–41, 44.

59. See *Vine's Complete Expository Dictionary*, New Testament section, 528.

60. I borrow this interpretation from Walter Wink, *Jesus and Nonviolence: A Third Way* (Minneapolis: Fortress, 2003); see especially chapter 2. And as many readers may have guessed, I first heard about Wink's book from Rob Bell ("Calling All Peacemakers: Part 3," sermon, Mars Hill Bible Church, Grandville, Mich., December 17, 2006).

61. Noting that Jesus' audience consisted of people who were already being humiliated like this, one translation reads, "*When* someone slaps you ... *when* someone takes your shirt ... *when* someone makes you carry a load ..." (Wright, *Matthew for Everyone: Part One*, 49–50 [emphasis mine]).

62. Wink (*Jesus and Nonviolence*, 14) cites the Dead Sea Scrolls, 1QS 7, on this point. It states that even gesturing with the left hand "carried the penalty of exclusion and ten days' penance."

63. We might ask, wouldn't slapping someone with the left hand be even more of a disgrace? Not necessarily. Perhaps a left-handed backhand would be akin to someone today biting their opponent. It would be an undignified move on the part of those who considered themselves superior.

64. Again, this act is designed as a humiliation to keep the oppressed in their place.

65. Contrast Matthew 26:53 with all that took place on Good Friday.

66. John's gospel reads, "When the soldiers crucified Jesus, they took his clothes, dividing them into four shares, one for each of them, with the undergarment remaining.... 'Let's not tear it,' they said to one another. 'Let's decide by lot who will get it'" (John 19:23–24). See also Matthew 27:31; Mark 15:24; Luke 23:34.

67. See Matthew 27:31; Mark 15:20.

7

GLUTTONY AND THE PERSECUTED

1. In other words, my love is that which I am magnetically drawn toward — that which has my heart

2. Or even since their creation, since the tree was most likely a part of the garden before the creation of humanity.

3. The desire to "be like God" is not bad. In fact, *we were made to be like God*. Jesus told his disciples to "be perfect, therefore, as your heavenly Father is perfect" (Matthew 5:48). We are to love as he loves, to be holy as he is holy, and even to be wise as he is wise. It was the dark methods by which Adam and Eve pursued this end that were self-destructive.

4. Furthermore, given the West's persistent overconsumption, we are doing catastrophic damage to God's good world. The damage isn't merely pollution. It affects the ecology and so contributes to famine and the strength of natural disasters. Far from gluttony being a personal sin, it affects the entire planet.

5. Obesity is still a major problem today. While 18,000 children under the age of five die each day because they are malnourished (see page 91), 55 percent of adults in America are overweight, and nearly one in four American adults is considered obese. Such overindulgence represented 12 percent of America's health care expenditures in the late 1990s — $118 billion (see Worldwatch Institute, "Chronic Hunger and Obesity Epidemic Eroding Global Progress," March 4, 2000, *http://www.worldwatch.org/node/1672*). Thus we not only spend on excess; we spend ridiculous amounts fixing the mess created by our excesses.

6. Matthew 6:21.

7. See Generous Giving, "Statistics and Trends," *http://www.generousgiving.org/page.asp?sec=4&page=660*.

8. Luke 3:38.

9. So asked Pilate when Jesus said, "Everyone on the side of truth listens to me" (John 18:37–38.)

10. See 1 Corinthians 15:45.

11. See Matthew 4:1–11; Mark 1:12–13. "The wild beasts" is an image used only by Mark.

12. See Genesis 1:26, 28; 2:19–20.

13. Matthew 4:3.

14. Matthew 4:6.

15. Matthew's gospel reads, "Those who passed by hurled insults at him, shaking their heads and saying, 'You who are going to destroy the temple and build it in three days, save yourself! Come down from the cross, if you are the Son of God!'" (Matthew 27:39–40).

16. Matthew 4:9 (my translation).

17. See Matthew 26:30, 36–46; Mark 14:26, 32–42; Luke 22:39–46; John 18:1.

18. Genesis 3:19.

19. See Genesis 3:23–24.

20. See John 19:34.

21. See Matthew 9:14–17; Mark 2:18–22; Luke 5:33–38; note, too, that John the Baptist referred to Jesus as a bridegroom in John 3:29.

22. See Revelation 19:7–9; 21:2, 9–10.

23. See Mark 1:15; Matthew 22:2–14.

24. See Matthew 26:6–13; Mark 14:3–9; John 12:2–11; and it could be argued that the event in Luke 7:36–50 is the same story set earlier in Jesus' life. This is by no means certain, but the stories are so similar it isn't much of a stretch to suggest that Luke's account emphasizes different details to make a different point. For the sake of this chapter, I will assume that these stories depict the same event.

25. William Lane (*Commentary on the Gospel of Mark* [Grand Rapids: Eerdmans, 1974], 492) writes, "The value of the perfume … suggests it was a family heirloom that was passed on from one generation to another, from mother to daughter." John tells us that the perfume "was worth a year's wages" (John 12:5).

26. If we assume that the four stories are the same (if Luke's account [7:36–50] and John's [12:2–8] describe the same event), then Mary would have been a poor prostitute in a village on the outskirts of Jerusalem where the holy might slip away for a little indiscretion. Mary would have served such men. It would have been her only income. We might

see the perfume in her mother's jar as a tool of the trade. Thus, though the white jar was precious, she was wasting the gift inside. What an image! Note that both stories take place in the house of a man named Simon. As a final note, the story is about Mary the sister of Lazarus, not Mary Magdalene.

27. John 12:4–5 specifies that it was Judas Iscariot who objected.

28. Paraphrase of the accounts in Matthew 26:10–13; Mark 14:6–9; John 12:7–8.

29. Luke 4:18–19 records the words of Jesus as he quotes from Isaiah 61:1 in the synagogue in Nazareth.

30. Shakespeare ends *Romeo and Juliet* with the same picture. Seeing his beloved dead, Romeo dies. Seeing her bridegroom dead, Juliet dies. Jesus saw those he loved dead in sin, and he died. Those who have been freed from sin see their Savior and choose to die to themselves. In both cases, the lovers in death actually live.

31. This anointing was preceded by the Father's own anointing of Jesus at his baptism as the one commissioned by the Spirit "to proclaim good news to the poor" (Luke 4:18; Isaiah 61:1). Perhaps the anointing of Jesus is done by both his Father and his church, as represented here by Mary.

32. Matthew 5:10.

33. See Stephen Covey, *The Seven Habits of Highly Effective People: Powerful Lessons in Personal Change*, rev. ed. (New York: Free Press, 2004), especially part 4 on renewal.

34. This is my rendering of Matthew 5:10.

35. John 7:37. The remainder of this section tells the subsequent events recorded in John 8–9.

36. See Zechariah 12:10–13:1.

37. See Isaiah 12:3; 44:3; Jeremiah 2:13; 17:13; among others.

38. John 9:2.

39. John 9:11, 17, 33.

40. See John 9:35–38.

41. 1 Corinthians 13:12–13.

8

THE STORY GOD LOVES

1. See Genesis 5. "And then he died" is a reversal of God's repetition of "it was good" throughout Genesis 1.

2. Note Paul's own confession of this condition in Romans 7:7–24.

3. See Numbers 13–14.

4. Though the account of the eating of the grapes is not included in the text, we may certainly speculate that some people ate the grapes. Leaving them to rot would be unlikely. It makes sense to speculate that those making decisions for the Israelites in the desert, when considering the future of their nation, would have sampled the produce of the land set before them.

5. See Exodus 2:23–25.

6. God also gives us his Spirit, who, like a pillar of cloud by day and pillar of fire by night, guides us and comforts us with his presence. And he also gives us the Scriptures, which, like the law carried in the ark of the covenant, remind us of the hope we have and the eternal kind of life we are invited to live.

7. See Numbers 1–4; 26 (see 1:1 and 26:3 for location).

8. The psalmist, the apostle Paul, the writer of Revelation — even Jesus himself — use this image from Numbers to describe books in which the names of the living are accounted (see Psalm 69:28; Luke 10:20; Philippians 4:3; Revelation 3:5; 20:12, 15; 21:27).

9. Matthew 26:27–28.

10. Deuteronomy 30:19–20.

11. In fact, Matthew says that some of Jesus' audience came from "the region across the Jordan" (4:25), the very place where Moses delivered Deuteronomy, as though those listening to the Sermon on the Mount had, in hearing Jesus, crossed over into the Promised Land.

12. Revelation 21:4–5 (my translation).

13. Matthew 7:24–25.

14. See Luke 16:19–31.

15. See Matthew 5:21–30.

16. See Matthew 25:14–30; Luke 15:11–32.

17. See Luke 12:16–21.

18. See Genesis 3.

19. C. S. Lewis, *The Problem of Pain* (1940; repr., New York: HarperCollins, 2001), 129. It should be noted that Lewis probably holds to more of a metaphorical understanding of hell than an annihilationist one, which he rejects explicitly on pages 127–28.

QUESTIONS FOR DISCUSSION AND REFLECTION

INTRODUCTION
HOLES IN A GOOD WORLD

1. What value is there in Christians helping a secular neighborhood and its businesses to thrive?

2. Most people tend to think of sin as a *thing* and not an absence. Do you agree with Jeff's interpretation that sin is a void?

3. Spend some time reading and thinking about the parable of the sower (Luke 8:5–8). In what way does God want to fill the voids in our world through you?

1

PRIDE AND THE POOR IN SPIRIT

1. Can anyone escape pride? What does it look like to be truly humble? Jesus was confident, bold, and charismatic — so why wasn't Jesus proud?

2. How does our pride separate us from others?

3. Jeff claims that "Privacy + Time = Destruction." Do you agree?

4. If we are made to be in community, what does that look like for you?

5. How can recognition of our spiritual poverty lead us closer to God?

2
ENVY AND THE MOURNER

1. List five things you envy.

2. What is it that makes it hard to consistently be happy for other people's good fortune or success?

3. How is Tom's story a comfort to Trish? How can our suffering become a gift for others?

4. The person who envies and the person who mourns both lack something. How can this be a torment for the first and a blessing for the second?

3
SLOTH AND THOSE WHO HUNGER
FOR A LIFE MADE RIGHT

1. Is being slothful the same as being lazy? How would you define slothfulness?

2. Why wasn't the master in Jesus' story of the bags of gold content with the servant's *saving* and *protecting* what he was given?

3. If God is actively filling the voids in our world, why are there still holes (loneliness, pain, ignorance)?

4. Do you hunger and thirst for things to be made right? What kills this passion within us? What do you often want instead?

4

GREED AND THE MERCY GIVER

1. Are humans naturally greedy?

2. How can hoarding what we have actually leave us with nothing?

3. Does Jesus really ask us to give away everything we have? Our iPods, socks, mocha lattes?

4. How does mercy give life meaning?

5

LUST AND THE PURE OF HEART

1. Is lust always about sex?

2. Why is lust destructive?

3. What does it look like to see God in others?

4. What kind of strength is found in overcoming lust? What can this strength do in your life?

6

WRATH AND THE MEEK PEACEMAKER

1. Is there ever a time when it is OK to be angry? Mull over possible examples.

2. How does Jesus' self-surrender defeat injustice when violence could not?

3. What are the primary characteristics of a child of God? What does it mean to inherit the earth?

4. Is violence ever the answer in the Christ-following life?

7
GLUTTONY AND THE PERSECUTED

1. Are overeaters the only gluttons?

2. How did Jesus succeed where Adam failed?

3. What are you united to?

4. Is there anything significant you need to sacrifice because of your love for God?

8
THE STORY GOD LOVES

1. Are you presently allowing God to restore your life?

2. Why do those who know they are loved by God sometimes return to the slavery of sin?

3. Where do you see the fruit of God's renewed world around you?

4. Specifically, how would you live differently now if you saw heaven breaking into this life?

5. How can you take the ideas from *Seven* and apply them in your life so that it becomes more than just "a book I read and put back on my shelf"?

ACKNOWLEDGMENTS

My deepest gratitude and love go out to:

- Kelly — my smile, my strength, my love. You continue to make my life a playground.
- the people of Atlas and the Theology on Tap crew, without whom I'd be just another lonely man.
- Peter Kreeft, who first pointed out to me these pairings of the Beatitudes and the seven deadly sins. And Dante, who showed us that angels sing the Beatitudes over those whose lives are in shackles.
- Tom Wright, for showing me Jesus again. Rob Bell, whose work has been a refuge for me. And Dallas Willard, who understood what Jesus was doing with these blessings. Many will know that when things work right in this book, they were these men's thoughts first. The failures are certainly my own.
- Tim Coons, who believes without seeing and always seems ready to jump off the side of a cliff with me.
- Tom Vaughan and the people of the Living Church, who sacrificed so much to support me over the last few years.

SEVEN

- John Topliff, for inviting a confused kid with a shaved head to write a book. And Angela Scheff, who let me submit drafts over and over again.*

- Pete Schaffner, who took the time to love me.

- all my parents, who always believe in me more than I do.

- the people of Trailhead, Cherry Hills, and Church at Carbondale, for being my family and pushing me along.

- Doug Self, Jim MacArthur, and Steve White, who carved out time to read and comment on early drafts of this book.

- Trumpmotherjones. Brothers, the weird gig circuit called. It said it wants the funk back.

*And thanks for reading and taking all my endnotes seriously!

NOTES

NOTES